Psychology Revivals

Ability

Originally published in 1926, the first part of this book attempted to formulate a theory of ability in the light of recent experimental results of the time. It discusses the nature of intelligence and the problem of special abilities, and includes a study of some typical forms of genius. The second part gives an account of a three years' experimental study of special abilities in arts and science respectively, carried out upon university students. Samples of the tests employed are included. The results are presented in non-technical form. Victoria Hazlitt was a pioneer of experimental psychology, which was particularly significant as a woman in the early twentieth century. In many cases her work anticipated later developments in psychology by many years. Today it can be enjoyed in its historical context.

Ability

A psychological study

Victoria Hazlitt

Psychology Press
Taylor & Francis Group
LONDON AND NEW YORK

First published in 1926
by Methuen & Co. Ltd

This edition first published in 2013 by Psychology Press
27 Church Road, Hove, BN3 2FA

Simultaneously published in the USA and Canada
by Psychology Press
711 Third Avenue, New York, NY 10017

Psychology Press is an imprint of the Taylor & Francis Group, an informa business

Publisher's Note

The publisher has gone to great lengths to ensure the quality of this reprint but points out that some imperfections in the original copies may be apparent.

Disclaimer

The publisher has made every effort to trace copyright holders and welcomes correspondence from those they have been unable to contact.

ISBN: 978-1-84872-250-7 (hbk)
ISBN: 978-0-203-79627-6 (ebk)
ISBN: 978-1-84872-251-4 (pbk)

ABILITY

A PSYCHOLOGICAL STUDY

BY

VICTORIA HAZLITT, M.A.

LECTURER IN PSYCHOLOGY,
BEDFORD COLLEGE, UNIVERSITY OF LONDON

WITH TWO PLATES IN COLOUR
AND SEVEN DIAGRAMS

METHUEN & CO. LTD.
36 ESSEX STREET W.C.
LONDON

First Published in 1926

PRINTED IN GREAT BRITAIN

PREFACE

IN 1920 Dr. Beatrice Edgell suggested that the Department of Psychology at Bedford College should attempt an investigation of the abilities involved in the work of the University Faculties of Arts and Science respectively. The Council of the College was approached and gave permission for the students to be tested for the purpose of the investigation. As a result, all the incoming students were tested in each of the years, 1921, 2 and 3; and in 1922 and 1923 those who had been previously tested were re-tested. The work was made possible by the kind co-operation of colleagues who gave information with regard to the work in their particular subjects; by the students in the Psychology Department who helped to administer the tests; and, above all, by the hearty co-operation of the whole body of students who were tested.

A sample series of the tests together with an account of the experimental work will be found in Part II of this book. Part I is devoted to a theoretical discussion of the nature of ability. For the views expressed in this the writer alone is responsible. The views were developed as the result of an effort to relate present-day theories of intelligence to the experimental results. Part I was written after the experimental results were obtained, so that the value of the results is not affected by the validity, or otherwise, of the theoretical argument.

My first acknowledgment of indebtedness is to Dr. Edgell, who has given guidance, criticism, and encouragement throughout the work. I wish to thank the Council of Bedford College for permission to carry out the tests and the Principal and Registrar for help in organizing the experiment from the administrative side. I am indebted also to the Principal and Staff of St. Katherine's College for their kind co-operation in the experiment upon the effects of coaching. I owe very much to Dr. Margaret McFarlane for many valuable suggestions and for carrying out the experiment at St. Katherine's College, and to Miss M. Boole Stott for help with the statistical work.

BEDFORD COLLEGE
March, 1926

VICTORIA HAZLITT

CONTENTS

PART I

THE NATURE OF ABILITY

PART II

TESTS FOR UNIVERSITY STUDENTS

LIST OF ILLUSTRATIONS

ABILITY

PART I

THE NATURE OF ABILITY

CHAPTER I

INTRODUCTION

THE subject of ability is one that is only just beginning to be incorporated in the general study of psychology. Baldwin's *Dictionary of Philosophy and Psychology*, which was published in 1911, gives no definition of the term other than the theological, "The sinner's power, or want of it, to do what is good in the sight of God." Under the word, "tests," it gives an account of tests for a number of special capacities, but neither here nor elsewhere is there a discussion of the general problem of ability. At that date only a few psychologists were working on problems of ability, and even at the present time it cannot be said that there is a generally accepted body of doctrine with regard to it. The layman has a number of perfectly definite questions as to the nature of ability, its cultivation, its diverse forms and its relation to genius. The psychologist is only beginning to work upon these problems and it must be confessed that such partial answers as he has formulated have not given much satisfaction to the layman. The latter would exchange all the psychologist's measurements and analyses for one such suggestion as Sir James Barrie's, that ability is knowing how best to crack your walnuts. If only his prejudice could be overcome, he would soon realize that the psychologist's measuring and analysing is full of the fun of the chase, and that to find out how people crack their walnuts, why some do it better than others, and whether the same crackers will crack all walnuts is in itself an absorbing pursuit. The facts that are now available seem to suggest certain answers to these problems, but as psychologists are not agreed on these answers it becomes necessary to review the position and to attempt a discussion of certain theories that have been put forward.

Current Views of Ability

During the present century a body of facts with regard to ability has been accumulated as a result of the application of tests to children and adults. The work which has led to this has been motivated by both practical and theoretical interests. In some cases it has been undertaken in order to discover the individuals best fitted for some given employment, in others the object has been to analyse ability as such. The two lines of inquiry are intimately connected; theoretical assumptions underlie the methods adopted in testing for practical purposes and the results of tests undertaken for practical purposes react upon theory. Much that is psychologically important may be learned from the history of the development of tests of ability, but as this history has been given elsewhere[1] it is possible to omit it here and to proceed immediately to an outline of the present-day views of ability. The view that is most generally held is that ability is an inherited mental capacity or group of capacities. The results of repeating tests on the same individuals at different ages tend to favour the view that the degree of this capacity present in a given individual does not alter with age. A child who

[1] See Ballard, *Mental Tests*. London, 1920. Spearman, *The Nature of Intelligence*. London, 1923. *Psychological Tests of Educable Capacity*. H.M. Stationery Office, 1924.

gives evidence of unusual ability at seven will almost certainly give evidence of unusual ability at seventeen. There is a tendency amongst psychologists to consider this capacity fully developed well before the end of the adolescent period. On this view the youth of seventeen or eighteen may be handicapped by lack of experience, but not by the absence of any fundamental ability in applying the knowledge that he has.

With regard to the nature of ability several problems arise. Is ability a unitary capacity of mind that will manifest itself indifferently whatever be the particular material with which the individual is working? In other words, is the person who is clever in one form of activity likely to be clever in another? Most modern psychologists consider that there is some general factor or group of factors in ability, and that the individual who has the general factor to an unusual degree is likely to do well in a range of subjects, but evidence is accumulating which shows that such an individual may lack a given special ability, and this lack may lead to his being outstripped in a special line of activity by others who have considerably less general ability. The existence of *idiots savants*, men who lack general ability to such a degree as to be distinctly subnormal and who are yet "geniuses" in some narrow branch of activity lends colour to the view that special abilities are of importance. The "genius" of Earlswood was incapable of looking after his own affairs, he was extraordinarily lacking in foresight and common sense, and yet he had wonderful manipulative skill and could plan and execute models of ships which showed him to be an expert craftsman, as well as a man of originality within a narrow sphere.[1] He is an outstanding example, but there are many other cases which resemble his more or less closely.

It is generally recognized that an individual who has even outstanding ability may fail from the lack of such qualities as perseverance, and that the possession of such

[1] Tredgold, *Mental Deficiency*. London, 1922, pp. 340–5.

moral qualities may lead to the success of the less gifted person.

The psychological investigation of special abilities is in its very beginning. Up to the present it has followed two main lines: the study of school subjects in relation to special ability or defect, and the study of special industrial tasks with a view to selecting those who show marked ability for them. With regard to school subjects, Dr. Burt puts forward tentatively the view that the five most important capacities are the following: [1]

1. Arithmetical Ability.
2. Linguistic „ (*a*) verbal, (*b*) literary.
3. Manual „
4. Artistic „
5. Musical „

The results of vocational testing have not led to the establishment of a number of special abilities such as these, but they show clearly that any given industrial task is likely to be better done by some people than by others, and that satisfactory tests for selecting those specially fitted for a given task can be framed. It has been suggested that there are in addition to general and special abilities, group factors, which influence the individual's performance in a number of special activities. Evidence for such group factors has not been established. The subject will be discussed in a later section (see p. 44 f.).

This view of ability as involving a general factor with a number of specific factors raises very many difficulties for the speculative psychologist. In face of the difficulties he is often inclined to be petulant with the experimentalists for presenting him with an array of ill co-ordinated facts, instead of being grateful to them for giving him bones to pick. The difficulties will be considered under the two main headings of "general capacity" (chapters II–IV), and "special abilities" (chapters V–VII). "General

[1] *Psychological Tests of Educable Capacity.* H.M. Stationery Office; cf. also Burt, *Educational Abilities*, p. 59.

capacity" is here substituted for the current term "general ability" because apparently all who believe in a general factor would agree that it can only manifest itself in the form of ability through special channels. In other words, if there is anything general it is a capacity; all abilities are special.

CHAPTER II

GENERAL CAPACITY

Divergence of Views as to its Nature

MOST of the experimentalists say quite frankly that they do not know what general capacity is, but that they have tests that measure it. The paradox in their position is much more apparent than real. If the experimenter has a test which enables him to separate the individuals who, as a matter of fact, do well in a wide range of activities from those who do badly, he is justified in regarding that test as a test of general capacity. That he cannot define this general capacity is unfortunate from the theoretical point of view, but of little importance practically. In 1921 the *Journal of Educational Psychology* invited a number of psychologists to contribute their views of intelligence. The diversity of the definitions given, and of the opinions expressed, has provided a veritable charivari for other psychologists ever since. Below are four definitions which are fairly representative :

(1) Intelligence is the power of good responses from the point of view of truth or fact.

(2) An individual is intelligent in proportion as he is able to carry on abstract thinking.

(3) Intelligence is adaptability to relatively new situations.

(4) Intelligence seems to be a biological mechanism by which the effects of a complexity of stimuli are brought together and given a somewhat unified effect in behaviour.

It cannot be said that the definitions are completely

irreconcilable, but it is obvious that the criterion of intelligence that would be framed as the result of accepting one, would not necessarily be a satisfactory criterion according to the others. In as far as this is the case one would expect the theoretical disagreement to have practical consequences, but the truth of the matter is that no experimentalist troubles about his definition of intelligence when he is framing tests. He derives his sanction from the degree of correlation of his results with other measures of the individual's proved efficiency in life.

Some psychologists hold that there is one general factor which plays a part in determining a man's ability through a wide range of activities, and there are others who would not subscribe to this view. In a paper read at the Seventh International Congress of Psychologists, Prof. Godfrey Thomson defends the thesis that there is no such thing as general ability, no one factor which by its amount in a man determines his performances in general and is the sole source of correlation between them.[1] It may be said in parenthesis that those who believe in a general factor are not committed to believing that it is the *sole* source of correlation between different performances. In taking the position that he does, Prof. Thomson seems anxious to draw attention to the complexity of the conditions which determine a man's performance of any one task, rather than to insist upon the absence of any general factor.[2] For he proceeds to suggest that such a general factor may be the facility with which old responses can be hitched on to new situations, and the readiness with which a response is discarded, almost before it is begun, if it is going to prove unsuccessful. He concludes his paper with the sentence, "But it may be that nothing general is left at all." A discussion of Prof. Thomson's suggestion that the general factor in ability may be a facility for hitching old responses on to new situations will be included in a later section

[1] See *British Journal of Psychology*, Vol. XIV, 1924.
[2] For a consideration of his view with regard to Group Factors see below, p. 44 f.

(see p. 33). His suggestion that there is no general factor seems to be very largely a *jeu d'esprit* and need not detain us.

Since the publication of the Symposium on Intelligence, Prof. Spearman's book on the same subject has appeared.[1] For over twenty years Prof. Spearman has championed the view that there is a general factor in ability. In his introductory chapter he puts his view in the following words :

> "The continued success of the same person throughout all variations of both form and subject-matter . . . appears only explicable by some factor lying deeper than the phenomena of consciousness. And thus there emerges the concept of a hypothetical general and quantitative factor underlying all cognitive performance of any kind."

This general factor is taken tentatively by Prof. Spearman to be the equivalent of energy or power. Each different cognitive operation is served by a specific factor peculiar to it, and Prof. Spearman suggests that this specific factor may be the correlate of the functioning of the specific neurons serving the particular kind of operation. He considers that general ability or intelligence cannot be defined in terms of any one psychological process, and he gives a very clear and searching criticism of the attempts that have been made to do this. One may readily agree that ability has not been satisfactorily defined in terms of psychological processes and still feel that Prof. Spearman's own theory of a general energy working a number of specific engines is extraordinarily difficult. It would seem to involve the very type of localization of function that is being discredited,[2] for such localization of sensory and motor functions as has been established is far too general in character to account for the special abilities that appear to exist (see below, p. 51 f.). Further, there is the objection that in adopting such a view one is basing the whole theory

[1] Op. cit.
[2] See Head, "Speech and Cerebral Localization," *Brain*, 1923, pp. 424–5.

of abilities on two unknowns, viz. "general energy" and "specific engines."

When he is dealing with intelligence from the descriptive side, Prof. Spearman says that it involves all the processes which come under his three neogenetic principles: apprehension, eduction of relations, and eduction of correlates. Presumably the special abilities may be distinguished by the material with which they deal, as their neuron localization is unknown. At this point we come upon a feature of Prof. Spearman's view of general and special factors in ability that brings him into line with practically all the other writers on the subject—they associate the general factor with psychological processes, while defining each special factor in terms of the material with which the activity is concerned. It will be suggested later that this affords a clue to the solution of the problem of general and special factors in ability.

Another clue to the solution of that problem may possibly be found in an examination of the tests which purport to be tests of general ability. The two tests which have had the greatest popularity for this purpose are the Prose Completion and the Analogies Tests.[1] Prof. Burt has found that a Reasoning Test is also a good test of intelligence. Dr. Ballard claims that the detection of absurdities may be used. A very brief consideration of these tests shows that they have a number of characteristics in common. The material with which they deal is probably the commonest activity of man, using words in relation to thinking. The passages for completion, the analogies, etc., are chosen from fields of common knowledge and, where possible, touch a variety of interests. In all these tests there is a problem, holding for consciousness a gap which can be filled in through the working together of experiences that every normal person will have had. In other words, it is the organizing activity of mind that is essential in all these tests. "Organizing" is here used in the sense of "making into living being"—the gap is

[1] For examples of these tests, see Part II, pp. 107, 109.

filled out with what becomes living tissue of experience. The term "synthetic" would be used were it not for its implication of a mechanical process dealing with fixed and static elements.[1] Even what to subsequent reflection appears as analysis derives its motive from the organizing activity and is indeed one aspect of the organizing act; the plant cannot grow without assimilating substances from the soil, but no one would say that it analyses the soil. Dr. Ballard has put the matter very clearly in his article on "The Limit of the Growth of Intelligence,"[2] in which he concludes that "a factor in, if not the whole of intelligence, is the power to integrate experience." As the organizing act always takes place in response to the presence of a problem, we may say that intelligence is the problem-solving organization of mind. This does not limit intelligence to any one of the so-called levels of mental life (see pp. 14–16). For the infant, the recognition of a simple sensory experience may involve a problem and therefore the activity of intelligence, whereas, for the adult the recognition takes place automatically. The adult seems to perceive objects without there being any problem present to mind. There is ample evidence to show that this is only because the recurrence of the same objects[3] in his world has made recognition habitual. In addition to the evidence for this that comes from the child's laborious process of learning his world, there are two very important groups of facts that point to the same conclusion. The first group includes all the evidence that comes from pathology as to what happens in progressive disintegration of the mind. The recognition of sense data again becomes a problem, and that in inverse proportion to the patient's previous familiarity with the objects concerned. The second group includes all the evidence that comes from the perception and recognition of objects that have some novel character-

[1] Cf. Spearman, op. cit., pp. 140–1.
[2] *British Journal of Psychology*, 1921, pp. 140–1.
[3] Certain difficulties attend the use of the word "same" even in relation to the object, but the statement is relatively true.

istic. The experimenter who wore glasses to invert his world was conscious of problems for a time, then habit intervened as it does for the child, and he seemed to see his world in order without any effort. If you look at any common object from a new angle or in a new relation you will realize that immediately the results of habit are partially eliminated, mental life is mainly concerned with the facing and solving of problems. The most fundamental appetites set the first problems, and these the week-old baby has begun to solve. As habit comes to rule in one field after another, so intelligence, the problem-solving organization, is free to conquer fresh territories.

The performance of the organizing act is mainly dependent upon two factors : (*a*) the drive which comes from the affective and conative setting of the situation, (*b*) the coming to consciousness of one or more elements relevant to the situation. This latter we shall call, provisionally, fecundity of ideas, but it will be suggested later that such a term is misleading (see below, p. 19). The organizing act is not completed without either an implicit acceptance of what comes, or an explicit judgment between alternatives. The judgment when it occurs consists in allowing the alternatives to develop their characteristics in relation to the given problem. This further process again involves the factor (*b*) above.

If this analysis is just it follows that the intelligent act involves two variables : (1) drive ; (2) what we are calling provisionally fecundity of ideas. It must be noted that while fecundity of ideas stands as one variable it includes two factors, namely, number of ideas and relevance of ideas. It is to be noted further that it is the qualitative factor of relevance rather than the quantitative one of number that is of importance. In very many cases the organizing act seems to be accomplished in a flash ; the one idea that comes is so perfectly adapted to the situation that there seems to be only one step in the solution. These cases illustrate to a marked degree the presence of an unconscious factor which is always operative ; the process involved in the rise to consciousness of the ideas related to the problem. The fact that this process may be assisted by certain devices of consciousness such as delay, dwelling on the problem in as many and as varied aspects as possible and the maintenance of a favourable emotional attitude, makes the process itself none the less unconscious. The drive cannot be regarded as an element in the organizing act as such. It is a pre-condition of intelligent, as it is of all other action that is not purely reflex. Its importance for the intelligent act is shown indirectly in James' remarks :

"I, who for the time have staked my all on being a psychologist, am mortified if others know much more psychology than I do. But I am contented to wallow in the grossest ignorance of Greek. . . . So we have the paradox of a man shamed to death because he is only the second best pugilist or the second oarsman in the world. That he is able to beat the whole population of the world minus one is nothing ; he has pitted himself to beat that one and as long as he doesn't do that nothing else counts." [1]

In as far as the degree of drive differs in the same person from one organizing act to another, the drive is presumably not the determinant of so-called general ability.

The second essential of the intelligent act, the essential which we have called provisionally fecundity of ideas, corresponds to the two processes which Prof. Spearman has called Eduction of Relations and Eduction of Correlates, but as in the first volume of his work he has set himself the task of writing about cognition without bringing in the problem of "Hormic Control," the subject of the relevance of the relations educed to the given task, does not arise. For instance he says, "The mentally presenting of any two or more characters (simple or complex) tends to evoke immediately a knowing of relations between them," and he gives the diagram :

[1] James, *Principles of Psychology*, Vol. I, p. 310.

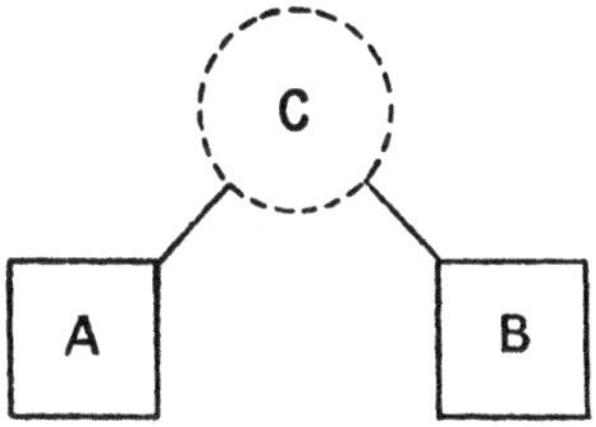

FIG. 1.—Spearman's Diagram to illustrate the Eduction of Relations.

Even such simple and diagrammatic characters as A and B, stand to one another in more than one relation, e.g. A = B, B is to the right of A, A is similar to B in shape, etc. Which of these relations shall be known when the two are presented? The essence of intelligence is knowing the relation which serves the purpose in mind, and if there is no purpose in mind it is unlikely that any relation will be known as the result of presenting the two characters. The same holds with regard to the Eduction of Correlates. This eduction of the relevant means that one part of experience is telling upon another; that not only does the presented character tend to come into relation with innumerable characters with which it has been associated in the past, but that the present task interpenetrates the whole situation.

INTELLIGENCE IS THE MEASURE OF CONFLUENCE OF EXPERIENCE

The thesis of this book is that intelligence is a problem-solving organization and that its efficiency is the measure of the degree to which experiences are confluent. In Figs. 2, 3 and 4, confluence is illustrated at three different levels. The effect of the background upon the rings in the illustration and of every colour upon every other that comes near it in perception is immediate and can be avoided by no effort of consciousness. The effects are believed to follow upon definite characteristics of the sense organ or

Illustrations of the Effects of Confluence at Different Levels.

The effects of confluence at different levels is illustrated on the following three pages.

Figure 2. Each of the horizontal pairs of rings is of identical colour and surface. Their apparent difference in colour is due to the effect of the backgrounds. This illustrates the effect of confluence at the so-called sensory level.

Figure 3. The two black figures are identical in size and shape The upper one looks smaller through the proximity of its smaller side to the larger side of the lower figure. This illustrates the effect of confluence at the so-called perceptual level

Figure 4. The identical word "fast" changes in significance in relation to its setting, and the setting is a significant whole only in relation to the reader's past experience. This illustrates the effect of confluence at the so-called conceptual level.

FIG. 3.—The Effect of the Surroundings upon the Perception of Size and Shape.

The FAST train.

The FAST set.

A FAST dye.

A FAST day.

Hold FAST!

FIG. 4.

nervous system, but the matter is far from clear. In Fig. 3 the influence of the one black shape upon the size of the other is immediate. It may, or may not, be more open to modification through experience than the colour contrast effect. Apparently no experiments have been performed to test if this particular illusion diminishes with practice; some spatial illusions do, others do not. It is to be noted that where an illusion disappears through practice in judging with knowledge of the results, no new factor is involved; all that has happened is that fresh experience of a corrective nature has been acquired and that this is effective in the later judgments. In Fig. 4 the word "fast" is affected by each of its contexts in a manner similar to the effect of one colour upon another and of one shape upon the shape near it. Each sentence is a whole for consciousness, and the nature of the word "fast" is as much affected by that whole as is the colour by its background.

It might be thought that the only effect of confluence at the ideational level would be to produce a confused broth of ideas, but this would be to overlook the fact that the problem itself is the determining element in the solution which comes from past experience; the different aspects of reality gained through experience check one another. For instance, if I am on a picnic and want to open a tin of salmon and find that the tin opener has been left at home how does my mind work? Inasmuch as opening something is the problem, I might draw out my latch-key, but I do not. Inasmuch as obtaining fish is concerned, I might hunt for a fishing rod, but once again I do not. I might heat the can to melt it, and so forth; there is no need to weary the reader with the list of all the futile things that I might do if the problem, the sealed can to be opened, did not immediately and without the need of rejecting all these farcical suggestions, draw from my past experience the one or two possibilities—such as using two stones—that fit the world in which that experience has been gained. It should be noted that the solution is not called forth by the fact that it is more habitual than the other possibilities; I have had no more experience of opening tins with flints than with latch-keys. In matters for which our experience has been inadequate, confluence may lead to our doing things as futile as those that have been mentioned as never occurring to us in the case of the familiar salmon tin. The child who oils the connections in an electric circuit to make the current run easily would not be called unintelligent. He shows a promising degree of confluence, he merely lacks experience.

In as far as problems are successfully solved experience grows in a fashion that fits reality, and the wider the experience the less the likelihood of confusion. For example, in the case of the word "fast" (see p. 16) no normal person is ever confused as to its meaning in a given setting. Difficulty would arise only if his experience had been inadequate. An unsophisticated child might quite well become confused through reading the meaning of "fast" as applied to a train in connection with "fast" as applied to set. Unless the individual has had the appropriate experiences and his mind affords the necessary degree of confluence for those experiences, no effort of his, no conscious process, can solve his problem intelligently, although, of course, there is always the possibility of his solving it unintelligently by persistence with varied effort. Even in this case the later efforts of the intelligent man will be more modified by the results of the earlier, than will those of the unintelligent man.

It seems unfortunate that in psychology the term "confluence" has been used almost exclusively in relation to a special group of illusions in which our tendency to be influenced by a figure as a whole leads to error in judging one of the parts. In the case of most illusions the confluence is admitted to be pre-psychological,[1] but it may certainly occur at different levels and, in any case, it is becoming increasingly difficult to know where the line between psychological and pre-psychological should be

[1] See, for example, Bates, "A Study of the Müller-Lyer Illusion," *American Journal of Psychology*, Vol. XXXIV.

drawn. It is strange that in treating illusions, psychologists have drawn a sharp distinction between contrast effects and cases of confluence. Obviously, the same cause is at the root of both, namely the tendency for one part of experience to influence another. For this phenomenon confluence seems to be the best term. That we are not making an illegitimate extension in the use of the term when we apply it to phenomena of intelligence, is suggested by the fact that when Prof. Stout is describing an outstanding case of the intelligent act, " confluence " is the term that he uses (see below, p. 66).

We have spoken of fecundity of ideas as the essential factor in intelligence, but it is now apparent that such a term implies both too much and too little. Too little, because it does not include the effect of confluence below the ideational level and also because it does not mark the fact that at the ideational level intelligence does not work by mere reproduction but by adaptation of past to present. Too much, because it suggests an explicit process of searching amongst a wealth or a poverty of reproduced items. An individual who is attempting to solve a problem may be reduced to such a search amongst a mass of more or less indifferent material, but this is not typical of the intelligent act. What is typical, is the comparative relevance to the situation of what comes. It is the unintelligent man, or the man faced with a problem too difficult for him to solve intelligently, who has to try one idea after another with little or no inkling of their suitability. Those psychologists who take the view that intelligence is a search amongst indifferent material, revive the old atomistic view of mind and usually imply the faculty hypothesis. Thus Prof. Claparède, in the Symposium at the International Congress, says :

" L'acte d'intelligence présuppose donc, pour être accompli, le concours de deux fonctions mentales différentes : *l'imagination* (qui suscite l'hypothèse), et les processus encore obscurs qu'on groupe sous le nom de *raison* (qui contrôlent l'hypothèse en la confrontant avec la réalité, ou avec les postulats posés).

Ces deux grandes fonctions, l'imagination et la raison, sont antagonistes, et jouent pour la pensée le même rôle que le ressort et le balancier dans un mouvement d'horlogerie. Le ressort, c'est l'imagination, qui tend à jeter dans l'esprit toutes les idées possibles ; le balancier, c'est la raison, qui règle les productions de l'imagination qui opère sur celles-ci une œuvre de selection." [1]

It is questionable whether even in the most passive moments of mental life there can be found evidence for an "imagination qui tend à jeter dans l'esprit toutes les idées possibles." Analysis seems to show that the freest associations and the idlest reveries have something corresponding to the "problem" of the intelligent act (it may be only the maintenance of a certain emotional mood), and that this determines what shall come to mind. In other words, even in these cases selection has taken place as an integral part of the "imaginative" act.[2] Similarly in the intelligent act, to envisage the problem, is to select what shall come to mind. Watt has shown that this is true and his results are repeatedly confirmed both in the laboratory and in every-day life.[3] The fact that the selection is an unconscious process is very well illustrated in the following passage from Helmholtz's "Autobiography":

" . . . as I have often been in the unpleasant position of having to wait for lucky ideas, I have had some experience as to when and where they came to me which will perhaps be useful to others. They often steal into the line of thought without their importance being at first understood; then afterwards some accidental circumstance shows how and under what conditions they have originated; they are present otherwise without our knowing whence they came. In other cases they occur suddenly without exertion, like an inspiration." [4]

In the case of very difficult problems the work of this fundamental process of selection is sometimes obscured because what comes does not solve the problem perfectly

[1] *British Journal of Psychology*, Vol. 14, p. 241.
[2] Cf. Edgell, *Theories of Memory*, p. 165.
[3] Watt, "Exper. Beiträge zu einer Theorie d. Denkens," *Arch. f. d. ges. Psych.*, Vol. 4.
[4] Helmholtz, "Autobiography" in *Popular Science Lectures*, Vol. 2, p. 283.

—the first solution and perhaps several others have to be discarded. No one would on reflection deny that there had been selection in these cases. The imperfection has been due to one or more of the following causes :

1. The problem may have been indefinitely or incorrectly envisaged.
2. Confluence may have been partial.
3. Necessary experience may have been lacking.

It is obvious that failure through the imperfections (2) and (3) is what would be expected upon the theory that intelligence is the measure of confluence. There may, however, be objection with regard to (1). If through envisaging the problem incorrectly or indefinitely I may fail to perform the intelligent act, is not "power of envisaging" a separate factor over and above degree of confluence ? Let us take a very simple concrete example in order to gain light upon this. A man is trying to solve a cross-word puzzle. His attempting to do it turns, as we have said, upon affective and conative factors which fall outside the subject of our discussion. Once he has undertaken it he must envisage problem after problem. One of these problems will serve as an illustration :

Clue—baked dough. Number of letters—four.

Having read "baked dough" he may begin immediately to fill in the word, "bread." If he does, he will have failed to solve his problem. Why ? Because the situation as a whole did not play its part. The problem was envisaged as, a-word-for-baked-dough instead of as, a-word-for-baked-dough-in-four-letters. His problem was too vaguely envisaged because there was a lack of confluence between the parts of his experience. When, finding that "bread" will not solve his problem, he envisages the problem as baked-dough-in-four-letters, "cake" may be configured as the solution. Once more he puts pencil to paper, but as he comes to the letter "a" he realizes that a few minutes before, he had decided that that space must be filled with the letter "o" because of what he had worked out with regard to the vertical clues. Thus once again his problem is corrected and made more precise through confluence. It becomes Baked-dough-in-four-letters-second-letter-o. This problem configures the correct solution " loaf." A man who actually went through all these steps would show relatively poor intelligence. His behaviour would approach the level of animals which come to the solution of their problems through persistence with varied effort.

Yet a further objection may be brought to the view that envisaging the problem does not introduce a second factor. It may be said that having envisaged a problem and failed to arrive at the solution, the individual may try different methods of arriving at his solution and that in his choice of methods, intelligence which cannot be equated to degree of confluence, may be shown. Here again a concrete instance may help. Suppose when the cross-word puzzle enthusiast came to the stage, baked-dough-in-four-letters-second-letter-o, no solution came, the situation would then become cannot-configure-solution-by-envisaging-problem. A fresh problem would then arise, ways-of-calling-words-to-mind. Once more the man's past experience will configure solutions to the problem, e.g.:

1. Look up " dough " in the dictionary.
2. Look through a cookery book.
3. Dwell on each of the letters of the alphabet in order.
4. Ask cook.

Whichever of these comes and is adopted, there will be a further change in the situation and a fresh problem will be envisaged. At this stage his intelligence will be again shown by the degree to which the original problem interpenetrates the subsidiary (cf. p. 37). The unintelligent person tends to solutions in which only a small part of the situation or of past experience has been effective. Cook says, " pie," and he runs off delightedly to write it down. He begins to go through the alphabet, " b " calls up " bun " and he begins to fill in the squares. He looks in the dictionary and seeing the word " paste," is just about to accept it, when finding that there are too many letters, he hurls the puzzle in the waste-paper basket. He has not solved his problem, i.e. accomplished the intelligent act, because all the essential configuring factors never once worked together—confluence was, in each case, partial.

We come then to the conclusion that trying and persevering only assist the intelligent act in the sense that they give the innate degree of confluence the opportunity to become effective. That they are not a general factor in intelligence is suggested by the fact that "plodding" and "persevering" are used almost universally for the innuendo "dull" and "unintelligent,"[1] and also by the fact that mentally defectives will often try very hard. They do not achieve success because they are usually lacking in experience, and because the experiences at their disposal are not confluent.

An experience which is fairly common in problem-solving has been quoted as a special objection to the view that has been outlined. Sometimes, when solving a problem, one feels that the solution which is still quite unknown must be along a certain track. For instance, a person is told that a picture at which he is about to look involves an absurdity or contradiction. Before looking at it he may think: "it will be to do with the shadows." With this idea in mind he may examine all the shadows to see if they are correctly orientated to the source of light. He may, or may not, find that they are wrong. The problem that concerns us is, how does the shadow hypothesis come? Many speak as if it were a kind of intuition, coming as a magical forecast of what will be found to solve the problem. But the shadow hypothesis is as much a product of past experience as any other solution of a problem. The problem, "wrong-with-a-picture?" configured "shadows" before the actual picture in question could take its share in modifying the solution. The hypothesis may have helped, or it may have hindered. All the shadows may have been examined in detail to the ex-

[1] Cf. Stout, *Analytic Psychology*, Vol. II, pp. 162–3.

clusion of other things. Having made sure that the shadows are correct, the observer may now look at the picture as a whole with the, "what's wrong?" problem in mind, and a gross error in perspective, or an anachronism in dress, may stand out immediately in consciousness as the solution of the problem. The hypotheses of the intelligent are more likely to help than those of the unintelligent just because they are the product of a higher degree of confluence. The intelligent man "knows" that the solution of his problem will lie along a certain line because configuration of the solution has begun.

At this stage it seems desirable to draw together the threads of our discussion by formulating definitions of certain terms that have been used.

Intelligence is the problem-solving organization of mind.

The General Factor in Intelligence is the measure of the degree to which experiences influence one another, or are confluent. The degree of this factor is determined by heredity.

Configuration is the unconscious process that is involved in the solution of a problem. It is the form that confluence takes in any given instance.

The term configuration is particularly associated with the Gestalt school of psychology. It is difficult to put the views of the Gestalt School into a general form, but it seems that their three main contentions are:

1. That consciousness is never the experience of a confused mass of qualities, but includes a background upon which qualities stand out in an orderly manner.

2. That no experience of an object is ever identical with another experience because the conditioning factors are infinite and are always changing.

3. That the influence of these factors is according to law.

The first of these claims emphasizes the result of the fact that consciousness is always concerned with a problem. All that is not part of the problem forms the background. The problem sets in relief the qualities with which it is concerned. This fact has been so obscured by our inveterate habit of thinking of consciousness as dealing with fixed and unaltering elements that it is very difficult to realize how important an influence the problem has upon what is perceived, and upon how it is perceived. What is meant by this may be made clear from an incident that occurs in the Chaplin film, "The Gold Rush." Two men, Charlie with his fluttering movements and inconsequent air, and a big brawny Scotsman of serious mien are confined to their hut for days by terrific storms. They are starving. The Scotsman is desperately hungry. He sits by the table with his head bowed in utter misery. Then he looks up at Charlie who has sat down opposite to him. His hunger problem transforms the inconsequent Charlie into a fully-fledged chicken. He sees Charlie as a chicken. This, it will be said, was an illusion or a hallucination and falls outside the field of normal perception. It was hallucinatory and the hungry Scotsman soon realized this, for as he gazed more steadfastly the chicken gave place to the fluttering Charlie again. Reality did not continue to support the perception that the urgency of his hunger problem had wrung from it. Let us compare this with a case which at first sight seems to be on an entirely different plane. Lister had been consumed with the desire to solve the problem of preventing and curing gangrene in wounds. His experiences were similar to those of other hospital surgeons, the world over, and his knowledge of Pasteur's work was shared with a very large proportion of the medical profession. The following is what his biographer says:

"Lister saw a vision of countless enemies awaiting the paralysis of the living tissues unprotected by the skin just as the vultures await the paralysis of a dying beast before they begin their fell work. Lister was almost certainly the only man in the world to whom that vision was as peculiarly vivid. He saw the very refinements and details of the drama that would occur between the tissues and their enemies." [1]

[1] *Lord Lister*. T G. Wrench, 1913, p. 103.

To a large proportion of his contemporaries, this vision was as much a hallucination as the Scotsman's chicken.

FIG. 5.—The Effect of the Problem upon what is Perceived.

Lister, himself, could not be sure that it was not a hallucination until he tested whether or no reality would support the vision. It may be objected that in this case the term vision can be used only metaphorically, that there is no change in perceptual experience such as was involved in seeing the chicken. There is some truth in this, although probably not as much as some would have us believe. The answer to such an objection is that where mental life deals with the solving of problems the perceived, the imaged, and whatever is thought in any other possible form, cannot be put into watertight compartments. Their interplay is infinite. Glance at the lines on p. 26. For most people they are a medley of lines and remain so for a few seconds, but the effort to see them as a whole succeeds and they undergo a kaleidoscopic change into a very characteristic picture. This surely is a case of perception with no question of hallucination or other pathological phenomena, and yet the change that the lines undergo in response to the demand for seeing them as a whole is identical in nature with the change of Charlie into a chicken. It is not uncommon for perceptions to have to be discarded through the urgency of the problem having led to a distorted view; the desired and expected friend who seems to be approaching turns out to be a stranger with a gait similar to the friend's gait, the ghost seen in the twilight twitches convulsively as only a cow's tail would twitch, and so forth.

The second contention of the Gestalt School, the claim that no experience of an object is ever identical with another experience, because the conditioning factors are infinite and are always changing, seems to be indisputable and is indeed bound up with the first contention. The third contention that the influence of these factors is according to law gives the only ground upon which a science of psychology is possible. When, however, Koffka and Köhler contend that the law is psycho-physical they seem to go beyond the evidence at present available. In our ignorance of the nature of both physical and psychical, their physical analogies seem at the best, futile; and at the worst, misleading. By using the term configuration, the present writer does not wish to be committed to the physical analogies of the Gestalt school, and this not from any philosophical prejudices as to the nature of the process, but as a matter of scientific principle.

The process of configuration has been recognized in varying degrees by most modern psychologists. The chapters on " Noetic Synthesis " and on " Apperception " in Stout's *Analytic Psychology* might be headed " Configuration," if but a very few alterations were made. The main difference between Prof. Stout's treatment of the subject and that of a writer such as Koffka, is that the former in talking of " mental systems " and in stressing the part played by language, seems to be ignoring that very plasticity for which the latter is contending. This is only a superficial view, however, for Stout tells us that Apperception " is the process by which conation fulfils itself," so that all the systems of which he speaks are mind as constituted by its solution of problems. He uses the term, " apperceptive systems," but it is obvious from all that he says that he does not mean this to imply anything static.

How little the mind is organized according to the categories of language and logic, is shown by the fact that most people would find it difficult to give even an approximate definition to innumerable words that stand for ideas that function, and function successfully, in everyday life. Further, there is a very characteristic difference between the experience of merely talking and of expressing thoughts as they develop. In the former case, the language mechanism repeats habit-formations, all goes smoothly but nothing new results. In the latter, speech is liable to be halting and often there is no appropriate word for the new thought creation. In discussing the bias towards formal logic in psychology, Prof. Ward says, " It is, as we have seen, the characteristic of every completed concept to be a fixed and independent whole, as it were, crystallized out of the still-fluent matrix of ideas." [1] We may carry on

[1] Ward, *Psychological Principles*, p. 313.

Prof. Ward's metaphor and say that if such crystals form too readily and remain insoluble in the "still-fluent matrix of ideas," they hinder the life processes of intelligence.[1] The fact that scholasticism contributed so little to the progress of human knowledge suggests that systematization is not the essential for such advance. "Actual thinking is always more or less rhapsodical and heuristic."[2] It has this character to our consciousness because we have no conception of the complexity of the matrix of ideas, nor of how aspects of experience, extremely diverse, may come together, a new creation, in the service of the problem of the moment. The Associationist School tried to find the links and to classify them according to formal categories. Their failure was conspicuous. The modern psychologist has given up the attempt. Even he, however, often writes as though ideas organized themselves on a linguistic, or at least, a verbal basis, and as though the process of thinking waited upon the possibility of explicit formulation. Such a view is notoriously false even to human experience, in which habit has undoubtedly made thought very dependent upon language as a tool. Judging from recent studies of the higher apes, they, at least, can think and solve problems successfully without the use of words.

[1] This fact is illustrated from many different points of view in Ogden and Richards' *The Meaning of Meaning.*

[2] Ward, op. cit., p. 327, note.

CHAPTER III

GENERAL CAPACITY (*continued*)

Illustrations of the Dependence of Intelligence upon Confluence

THAT confluence is a verifiable phenomenon, accountable for illusions will be allowed by every one, but few, if any, take account of it as a factor in all experience. As Pillsbury says, only when the processes that ordinarily give rise to what we call true perceptions give rise to false results, is our attention called to them. Prof. Spearman devotes some space to discussing confluence in relation to illusions. He is chiefly interested in the special case of the erroneous identification of thought process with miscellaneous movements, but he illustrates the existence of confluence over a wide range of experience and quotes in particular the Müller Lyer illusion as an instance (see Fig. 6). The significant fact for our purpose

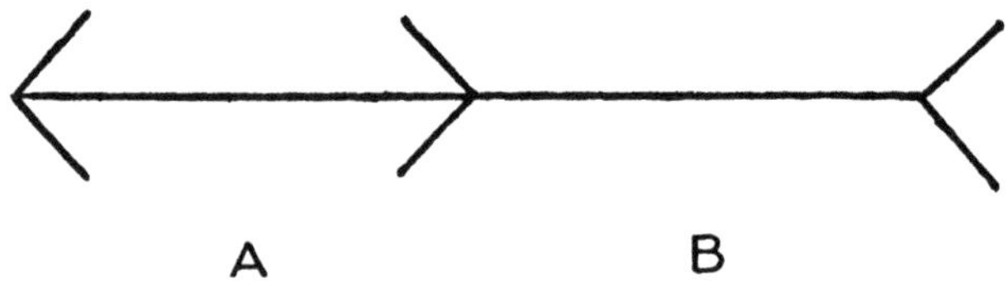

Fig. 6.—The Müller Lyer Illusion. The horizontal lines A and B are equal in length. Normal people see line B as considerably longer than line A.

is that intelligent children have the illusion, mentally deficient children do not. In the case of the intelligent child the horizontal lines in A and B respectively are interpenetrated by the effect of the oblique lines; in the case of the mentally deficient, each line stands in isolation and there is no modification of the horizontals by the form of the figure as a whole. That the illusion is due to confluence is shown by the fact that if the horizontals are coloured differently from the obliques, or in other ways confluence is checked, the illusion is reduced. The integration upon which the illusion depends takes place at a lower level than the level involved in intelligent action, but the results are the same. The Müller Lyer figure is a case in which confluence gives rise to difficulties. In most problems it favours the finding of a solution. Thus in Terman's test for nine-year-old children in which the problem is to bring the words, boy, ball, river, into a sentence, the normal child reads the three words, and as he reads them in order, his idea of each one is modified by the others so that as a result he is able to conceive a thought in which the three come into a unitary relation, The boy dropped his ball into the river, etc. The mentally deficient child either repeats the words and can conceive no connection, or frames a sentence which does not comprehend all the three ideas. The following sentences were given by mentally deficient children who were all over nine years of age:

(*a*) A ball is for kicking.

(*b*) The boy goes and plays with another boy.

(*c*) The boy was playing with a football. River. The boy was fishing for fishes in the river.

(*d*) Boys run.

(*e*) Boys kick ball and swim in the water.

(*f*) The boy goes to school, the ball's for playing with. (Given by a woman of twenty-three.) [1]

These sentences illustrate what Bleuler has remarked with regard to the imbecile's difficulty in forming concepts,

[1] For these examples I am indebted to the kindness of Miss E. Ross, Inspector of Schools for Mentally Deficient Children under the London County Council.

"the imbecile does not view simultaneously the structure of colour, form, and position (of a leaf) and therefore shows a tendency to ignore some individual components and to overestimate others." [1]

No one has done more to draw attention to the fact of confluence than Prof. Koffka, although he does not use the term. His "configurations" are patterns formed by confluence.[2] He deals with cases such as those illustrated on pp. 14–16. He shows how every experience of a thing differs however slightly from every other, because in each the whole changing experience of the individual has come into relation with, and tinged the element which is under consideration. The comparability of this phenomenon with what occurs in other spheres of experience is brought out very clearly by him in his references to experiments on problem-solving by animals and human beings. He says:

> "The nature of the subject's understanding is described by Rüger in detail. It is not at all a process limited to human ideas, but is one that can take place entirely at the level of perceptual phenomena; in which case the *perceptual material undergoes a transformation*, often sudden and profound, without in any way involving the introduction of ideas." [3]

Transference is only another instance of the same phenomenon. In speaking of one of Köhler's chimpanzees which, having learned to use a stick to draw fruit into his cage, used his blanket in the same way when the stick was missing, he says:

> "As Köhler expresses it, the stick as it appears in the field of vision has acquired a definite functional value in certain situations,

---

[1] Bleuler, *Text-Book of Psychiatry*, 1924.

[2] It is difficult to give a brief quotation to support this, but it is implied several times in the course of the chapter on "Behaviour and Learning" in *The Growth of Mind*. For example, in talking of the solution of a problem he says, "What we should say is that an intelligent construction of the field takes place with respect to the goal, and that the solution is nothing else than the arousal of this construction," p. 209.

[3] *The Growth of Mind*, p. 177.

and this effect in itself is *carried over* to any object which may have certain general characteristics in common with sticks, even though these objects appear otherwise quite different." [1]

The "transformation" of the perceptual material and the "carrying over" of the functional value are perfect analogues of what takes place in the Müller Lyer figure—they are cases of confluence. The example of the chimpanzee may recall the view suggested by Prof. Godfrey Thomson that the general factor in ability may be facility in hitching old responses on to new situations. The chimpanzee's "old" response is hauling fruit by means of something used as a tool, the "new" situation is "blanket as only possible tool." But here we come upon the difficulty in Prof. Thomson's view. It is obviously not the old response that is hitched on. It is a response of a fundamentally different nature through its adaptation to the new situation, so different that an animal less intelligent than a primate would almost certainly fail to carry over the effect. In other words it involves a high degree of confluence. The only sense in which it can be called the same response is that it attains the same end. Physiologically it is very different. Failure to note this commits one to the synthetic, instead of the organic view of mind.

The study of animal behaviour shows that "carrying over" may be very difficult, or even impossible for lower animals, in cases in which it would take place immediately in higher. An example of this was shown by a cat recently observed. This cat, like most of his kind, is very fond of chicken bones, but they are a treat which he does not frequently enjoy. On one occasion he was very hungry and on smelling his usual fare mewed lustily. He was given some chicken. Although his eyes were directed towards the chicken, he did not see or smell it, but continued to mew. The functional value of his usual fare was not carried over to an object which, apart from his

[1] *Ibid.*, p. 192.

occupation with the other smell, would have had the preference. Finding that his mewing did not bring the expected food, he went away to return a little later and eat up the chicken with great avidity.

Evidence for the dependence of intelligence upon degree of confluence may be deduced from a fact that is well known with regard to the use of tests. It is well established that any one kind of test is most useful in grading a group according to their intelligence on its first application. The connections that are appropriate for solving the problem can be made even by the dullard if he has a second or third opportunity. As any given kind of material becomes familiar (this is not assuming that the *same* test would be given to a group more than once) relevant connections spring into mind much more easily than they did when it was unfamiliar. Bleuler, who uses the phrase " frequency of associations " for what we are terming confluence, says :

> " Yet to a certain extent number of associations can be replaced by the frequency of the experience. Thus the perceived details . . . may suffice to form a distinction even when there are relatively few associations, if the sensations are constantly repeated in a way that now one, now another detail will become firmly associated with the problem. To be sure an animal rich in association will acquire right at the first experience all the connections necessary for the particular purpose." [1]

The advantage of the intelligent person lies in the fact that his " make-up " favours confluence even when the material is relatively new. From this comes the essence of Stern's definition of intelligence, that it is adaptability to the new problems and conditions of life. In an earlier section it was noted in passing that the tests of general capacity which are in common use have for their material the most familiar subjects and the commonest activities. On the theory that intelligence is the measure of the degree of confluence, this is what would be expected because, inasmuch as familiarity favours confluence, differing

[1] Bleuler, *Text-Book of Psychiatry*, p. 597.

degrees of familiarity with the material amongst the testees would mask the effects of the innate quality. The writer came across an interesting illustration of this. Ability to read matter in which the words are printed backwards has been claimed to be a good test of general capacity. One testee who had only very average capacity as judged by other criteria, did brilliantly on this test. It was discovered that while the other testees had never attempted such a thing before, this one had practised it from the time when as a child she was struck by the strangeness of the word Mazawattee, and with great difficulty turned it into Eettawazam. In framing tests of general capacity, the problem before the psychologist is to frame tasks that are new, in material that is equally familiar to all the testees. The psychologist can never solve this problem perfectly in any one test and that is why it is advisable to have a number of different tests so that differing degrees of familiarity with the material may be compensated.

Degree of Confluence is the General Factor implied in the Current Definitions of Intelligence

In an earlier section (see p. 6) four fairly representative definitions of intelligence were quoted. If confluence is the general factor it should be possible to demonstrate that it figures in each one of these. "The power of good responses from the point of view of truth or fact," is dependent on all the relevant items being able to come together easily to configure the solution to the problem. In the second definition, intelligence is identified with ability for abstract thinking. Bleuler, who in his work has had a unique opportunity of studying the effects of lack of intelligence, says:

"The poverty of associations (low degree of confluence), impedes the formation of concepts because the latter naturally require a combination of many actual experiences and what is more they must be not only of the present but also of the past. The more abstract a concept the more combinations must be made." [1]

In other words, ability for abstract thinking is a criterion of intelligence because it involves to a high degree the factor that is essential for all grades of intelligent action. As a definition, the identification of intelligence with ability for abstract thinking seems too narrow, because, as we have suggested, intelligence may be manifested at the perceptual level. The third definition that intelligence is adaptability to new situations, has already been considered in relation to the present view. The fourth definition, that it is a biological mechanism by which the effects of a complexity of stimuli are brought together, is only another way of saying that it is the measure of confluence, although on grounds of language and of science we should prefer to call it a biological *organization*. The reference to a biological "mechanism" brings us to a further argument for the view that is being suggested.

A Consideration of Physiological and Biological Facts

Confluence is not only a verifiable fact on the psychological side, it has also an obvious correlate on the physiological, namely, plasticity of the nervous system and its integrative functioning. Prof. Koffka says that it is by virtue of his plasticity that man is superior to all other living creatures. It is equally true that men are differentiated amongst themselves by the degree to which they possess this same plasticity. Prof. Elliot Smith brings a wealth of evidence to support the view that man's evolution has depended upon the circumstances that led to the development of the mechanism which provides the physiological condition for confluence. He says:

"Life amidst the branches of trees limits the usefulness of olfactory organs; but it is favourable to the high development of vision, touch, and hearing. Moreover, it demands an agility and quick-

[1] Op. cit., p. 598.

ness of movement that necessitates an efficient motor cortex to control and co-ordinate such actions as an arboreal mode of life demands (and secures, by the survival only of those so fitted), and also a well-developed muscular sensitivity to enable such acts to be carried out with precision and quickness. In the struggle for existence, therefore, all arboreal mammals such as the Tree Shrews, suffer a marked diminution of their olfactory apparatus and develop a considerable neopallium, in which relatively large areas are given up to visual, tactile, kinaesthetic, and motor functions, *as well as to the purpose of providing a mechanism for mutually blending in consciousness the effects of the impressions pouring in through the avenues of the different senses.*" [1] (The italics are mine.)

"In learning to execute movements of a degree of delicacy and precision to which no ape could ever attain—and the primitive Ape-Man could only attempt once his arm was completely emancipated from the necessity of being an instrument of progression—the cortical area that is pre-eminently concerned with the phenomena of attention became enhanced in importance. Hence the pre-frontal region, where the activities of the cortex as a whole are, as it were, focussed and regulated began to grow until eventually it became the most distinctive characteristic of the human brain, gradually producing the distinctively human forehead. . . . However large the brain may be in Homo neanderthalensis, his small pre-frontal region is sufficient evidence of his lowly state of intelligence and reason for his failure in the competition with the rest of mankind."[2]

The cortex is a biological mechanism for confluence, and the growth of the cortex has been the most significant development in the most intelligent animals. Prof. Elliot Smith speaks of the pre-frontal area as pre-eminently concerned with the phenomena of attention. Most modern psychologists would be very glad to see the term attention disappear from psychology because it has been so much abused. It does, however, hold together, and stand for, a number of facts. In the light of what has been suggested with regard to the nature of intelligence, and of the theory advanced by Prof. Elliot Smith, would it not be possible to envisage attention as the degree to which a given problem interpenetrates the psychological situation? There are always problems, each tending to configure its own solution by means of the cortical mechanism through

[1] Elliot Smith, *The Evolution of Man*, p. 30.
[2] *Ibid.*, p. 41.

which both confluence and control of muscles and sense organs are gained. If one problem absolutely dominates, attention is concentrated. If there is rivalry between problems, attention is distracted or diffuse. In spontaneous attention the problem dominates without conflict owing to its consonance with the instinctive and affective setting of the moment. Involuntary attention exemplifies cases in which the situation gives rise to problems of deep biological significance which through their reflex prepotency interfere with problems of a higher stage of development. Witness the London policeman who threw the traffic into confusion as the result of having put on a new and ticklesome vest (*Punch*, 1925). In voluntary attention the problem of the moment dominates fairly successfully, for a time at any rate, in spite of the competition from other instinctively and affectively more favoured problems. It is able to do this because of its relation to a wider problem which has the pre-eminence. Thus voluntary attention involves a very high degree of confluence—the interpenetration of the present moment by one problem through its confluence with another. This results in an enhanced degree of selection with regard to the solution of the subsidiary problem. The man who dislikes climbing and is doing it only to cross the range to a distant town is likely to choose a shorter route than the man who cares for climbing as a pastime.

Expressing the matter in terms of the problem, brings out what is meant by the "focusing" and "regulating" of which Prof. Elliot Smith speaks, more clearly than the use of the word "attention," which in spite of a whole literature of protest is constantly used in such a way as to imply a more or less personified, selective agent. According to the view suggested attention is the measure of the degree to which the problem interpenetrates the mental life of the moment. As this aspect of confluence is very important for intelligence, it is not surprising that power of voluntary attention, which involves the highest degree of confluence, has been suggested as a measure of intelligence. It seems probable however, that while no one who lacks power of voluntary attention can be very intelligent, there may be some who have good powers of attention, and who yet do not show exceptional intelligence. In them the task in hand may dominate all that comes to mind, but their solutions do not involve a high degree of confluence in their experience as a whole. Apart from this, it is difficult to see how power of voluntary attention could be taken as the measure of intelligence, because some will attend spontaneously to problems which demand voluntary attention from others.

The conclusions of all recent workers on the physiology of the cortex favour the view that it is a comparatively non-specialized mechanism which brings the organism into relation with the whole of its environment through the distance receptors, and which provides the essentials for an almost infinite number of connections and relations. Thus Dr. Head says:

"The processes which underlie an act of speech run through the nervous system like a prairie fire from bush to bush; remove all inflammable material at any one point and the fire stops. So, when a break occurs in the functional chain, orderly speech becomes impossible because the basic physiological processes which subserve it have been disturbed. The site of such a breach is not a centre for speech but solely a place where it can be interrupted or changed.

"Most so-called centres in the nervous system are strictly speaking nodal foci, where central neural activities undergo integration and other changes in relation to one another. Like the points on the railway, they determine the subsequent course of events. This may happen automatically or voluntarily, just as the passage of a train may set the track for its successor, or the mechanism may be manipulated at the will of the man in the signal box in response to information received from without. Such a 'centre' also forms a shunting station where one group of impulses is guided in one direction, whilst another passes on into some fresh combination.

"Whenever a primitive function is rendered more perfect and given a wider range of purposive adaptation the structures which are primarily responsible for its existence become linked up with those on a higher anatomical plane of the nervous system. But many of the more mechanical processes and the actual force expended may still be furnished by the lower functional levels. No fresh 'energy' is generated by this higher integration, but the response gains in freedom; it can be more closely regulated according to the needs of the moment and brought into harmony with the reactions of the organism as a whole. This is the purpose of the series of complex integrative changes which start with the birth of afferent impulses at the periphery and continue until their ultimate consequences act on the final efferent path." [1]

[1] Head, "Speech and Localization," *Brain*, 1923, pp. 424–5.

CHAPTER IV

GENERAL CAPACITY (*continued*)

Intelligence does not Develop

IF the view that has been outlined is justified, it follows that it is a fallacy to talk of the development of intelligence. The first organizing act of the child differs in no way from that involved in the profoundest discovery of the scientist or philosopher. There is no development of a process; there is merely the acquisition of experience which, according to the innate grade of intelligence of the individual, can interact more or less with other experience. Such a view as this is sure to meet with opposition. The ordinary adult dislikes such a view, because, misinterpreting it, he concludes that he has lived in vain—it is quite amusing to watch the effect of telling a class of adults that intelligence does not develop after the age of sixteen, or whatever other age has most recently been made the limit! The experimental psychologist says that intelligence must develop because he can determine the point at which it ceases to develop. To the adult's dislike of the theory we need pay no serious attention, but we may try to answer the experimentalists' objection. Until the child has reached the adolescent years he does not develop all the interests of the adult. This means that before this period there are gaps in his experience which make intelligent action in certain spheres, and with regard to certain matters, impossible.

As soon as these gaps are filled, there is no greater distinction between the adult and the adolescent than there is between one adult and another. This agrees perfectly with the experimental results and fits in well with instances of child precocity which would be much more difficult to understand if intelligence were a function which develops gradually. It is significant in this connection that Mr. Hugh Gordon has found that the intelligence quotients of children tend to vary according to the degree of their regularity of attendance at school and that the intelligence quotients of the children of gipsies and bargees become lower as the children grow older.[1] It is unlikely that such children fail to develop any normal form of mental process, but it is quite certain that they do not gain the experiences essential for making readily the connections involved in solving the test problems.[2] This will necessarily lead to the lowering of the intelligence quotient as they grow older. If some one could frame a graded series of tests founded on the little bargees' experiences and activities, is it likely that their intelligence would appear to "wither and fade" with age?[3] The increasing use of tests of intelligence in schools makes this problem of fitting the test to the child's environment a very real one. A teacher from an elementary school in a very poor neighbourhood gave an example of how very difficult it may be for the outsider to realize the limitations imposed by certain environments. An inspector came to the school and was particularly interested in testing the children's ability to solve problems in mental arithmetic. He gave what seemed to him the problems with which the children would be continually faced in running errands. He spoke of "half a pint of milk," a "pound of rice," etc. The teacher in commenting upon this explained that none of

[1] Mental and Scholastic Tests among Retarded Children, Board of Education.

[2] Since this sentence was written experimental proof for the view expressed in it has been published. See Frances Gaw, "A Study of Performance Tests," *British Journal of Psychology*, Vol. 15, Part IV, pp. 389–91.

[3] Cf. Ballard, *The New Examiner*, p. 120.

his problems had the background that he assumed because most of the children buy in "pennorths." It is obvious that such a lack of adjustment in a psychological test would not only give a false view of the intelligence of the group as a whole, it would also put the few more fortunate who buy by quantity at an unfair advantage. The situation would be analogous to marking one half of a group taken at random on the problems they could solve in terms of chains, furlongs, and miles, and the other half on problems involving pounds, shillings and pence. Those who had the old familiar pounds, shillings and pence would appear, on the average, very much more intelligent.

With regard to the development of intelligence, then, we may say that no one has succeeded in demonstrating stages of advance that cannot be explained as due to the gaining of familiarity with particular kinds of material. In the next two chapters this view will be developed in relation to the theory of so-called special abilities.

CHAPTER V

SPECIAL ABILITIES

THE PROBLEM OF THE EXISTENCE OF SPECIAL PSYCHOLOGICAL ABILITIES

EVEN if it be agreed that intelligence is a unitary function of the form that we have described, the possibility of there being, in addition, special abilities, is not necessarily precluded. The crucial problem with regard to special abilities is, "Are they determined by special psychological processes, or are they solely dependent upon differences in the material with which they deal?" There is an absolute lack of evidence for special psychological abilities. Thus Dr. Burt says:—

"Special abilities of a more elementary and strictly psychological kind have been found far harder to determine. As already observed, in supposing that definite faculties could be measured by one or two typical tests, the earlier experimenters proved to be much mistaken. The few recent inquiries that have approached the problem with the proper statistical methods—those of correlation and partial correlation—have so far been unfruitful: they have as yet succeeded in isolating no special unitary functions, much less have they succeeded in devising for such functions any specific tests." [1]

Prof. Godfrey Thomson maintains that there are group factors in intelligence. If these were proved to exist they would approximate to special psychological abilities. Prof. Thomson's position is, however, difficult to grasp.

[1] "Psychological Tests of Educable Capacity," *Board of Education Report*, p. 20.

He does not make any suggestions as to what the group factors are. He uses psychological tests for prognosis and thereby implies that what a child can do in tests (well varied, it is true) is a measure of what he will do in school work in the future. This leads to a view of the testees as graded according to the degree to which they possess a number of group factors, and this grading is the basis of the prognosis. At the same time, Prof. Thomson talks of a mental task being performed by different methods at different times, implying that on one occasion it might be performed, e.g., by the factors, 2A3B9Y, and on another by the factors A2D3Z.[1] Now are not these two positions, reliance on the tests for prognosis and admission that an activity may depend on different group factors at different times, mutually destructive unless the group factors are further determined by a general factor ? For apart from some such determination, a testee who solves the test problem successfully, using one combination of factors, may fail in similar work on all future occasions through using another combination. Further, there is in the position a still more fundamental difficulty, namely, the implication that every method of performing a task implies a separate factor in ability. It is the faculty hypothesis in its most exaggerated form.

There has been a fairly general tendency both in psychology and in popular thought to regard memory as a special psychological factor in ability. In order to discuss this view let us consider what is involved in a particular case of remembering. I learned " The Bard " when I was a child. I want now to recall it verbatim. There is present to my mind some symbol for what is to be recalled ; in a way, there is a problem, but we avoid using the term here because the gap involved can be filled by what has been already experienced, it does not call for a creation. If it is possible for me to remember the poem, thinking of the symbol will lead to configuration

[1] Cf. Thomson, " General Versus Group Factors in Mental Activities," *Psychological Review*, 1920.

of the parts of the poem in succession. But this sounds very much like the old story. We are back at the general factor in intelligence, for the configuration must depend upon confluence. Shall we say that memory and intelligence are one and the same function ? No, because the problem of recall does not involve the bringing together of experiences in forms in which they have not existed for the individual before. The clue to the difference between memory and intelligence seems to be supplied by the fact that people with very poor memory (as tested by a number of different tests), are much more likely to be lacking in intelligence than people with good memory are likely to have outstanding intelligence. From this one would infer that memory and intelligence are related but that intelligence involves either something in addition, or to a higher degree. In order to call up the past in the form that is characteristic of memory, confluence between present and past must be possible, but there need be little or no confluence between parts of the present situation, or parts of the past experience. For the intelligent act, however, this higher degree of confluence is essential. For instance, if my problem instead of the recall of " The Bard " had been a-poem-with-historical-reference-that-contains-a-good-example-of-alliteration, confluence would have been involved in bringing together poem, historical, alliterative ; a process that could not have been consummated in the defective or unintelligent mind. When this process has taken place, the possibilities for the solution of the problem are more numerous than in the case of memory and, therefore, once again, a higher degree of confluence is necessary. There can be no doubt that there are acts of so-called memory that very closely resemble the intelligent act. For instance, " When have I been amongst flora resembling this of the South Downs ? " The probability is that a continuous series could be made from the most stereotyped repetition, through all grades of solution, to the " discovery " of the highest act of intelligence. The typical act of recall would come somewhere in the middle of this scale. The persistence of habit-memory at the level where confluence is so low as almost to preclude modification in relation to the situation, is well illustrated in an example given by Bleuler. It is the case of a mentally deficient cook. She had learned to cook in a family of four. When she moved into a larger establishment she continued to cook four eggs for breakfast, although there were twelve to eat them.

Kind and degree of imagery are functions that have been regarded by some writers as turning on innate differences. Recent work on imagery tends to discredit the view that people belong to types with regard to their imagery. It seems that the kind of imagery used depends on the problem to be solved. Prolonged practice at solving some particular kinds of problems may lead to an individual having the imagery appropriate to such problems to a marked degree, but this gives no ground for assuming an innate endowment in that form of imagery. In the same way, an incapacity for certain forms of imagery may not imply an innate lack. The disability may arise from absence of appropriate experiences or from inhibiting emotional effects in the early years. Even if there are innate differences in kind and degree of imagery these would not account for the varieties of special abilities that are found (see p. 51*f*).

We have contended that in the case of memory no special psychological process is involved. We hold that this is true of all the so-called special psychological abilities. The process remains the same—problem envisaged, solution configured by an unconscious process dependent upon confluence. Most modern writers make it clear that they cannot draw any real distinction between imagination and scientific thought. There is no real psychological distinction. The only difference is that the activity that is usually associated with the term "imagination" has a different problem from that of the activity that is usually associated with "scientific thought"; but even in the kind of problem there could be made a continuous series from the "wildest flight of imagination" to the problem of the logician reflecting upon some scientific subject.[1] The most unconvincing chapter in nearly every textbook of psychology is that on thinking Either the writer says very little at all, or else he gives a more or less illustrated catalogue of typical problems, treating each one as if it involved a specific kind of mental process. He talks, for instance, of comparison. But comparison is only a name for those problems that deal with likenesses and differences. These problems configure their solution just as do any other problems. Prof. Stout in his *Analytic Psychology* has a chapter on Comparison and Conception, and what he says in it agrees very well with the view here taken. Thus he says:

> "In comparison we search for relations of likeness and difference, agreement and disagreement, between objects. It always occurs as a part of a more comprehensive process. It is subservient to the attainment of some ulterior end, theoretical or practical, and this end constitutes the impulse and incentive to it. The process itself involves a peculiar transitive movement of attention from one object of comparison to the other; the peculiarity of this mental transition is that attention remains as far as possible fixed on A, in the very act of fixing it on B." . . . "As the result of the process there emerges an apprehension of agreement and difference, together with a more or less sharp distinction between the points in which the objects agree and the points in which they differ."[2]

"The peculiar transitive movement of attention" is due to such subsidiary problems as what-is-A's-colour, what-is-B's-colour, being configured by the main problem. These two problems must configure their solutions in rapid succession or confluence between the two characteristics to be compared will become impossible and the difference will not be configured, unless, indeed, the situation is one in which language can keep the characteristics in question before the mind in a sufficiently exact form. That comparison as a faculty has taken longer than most to die is probably due to the fact that philosophy has harboured

[1] This view seems to have been entertained by F. H. Bradley, although at the time at which he was writing he had not the facts he desired. Cf. "Memory and Inference," *Mind*, 1899, p. 155.

[2] Vol. 2, pp. 168–9.

prejudices with regard to it. The prejudices have belonged to opposing schools, but they have equally led to a falsification of the psychological process. James' description of the facts and his discussion of their relation to the two antagonistic views in philosophy is classical. In the following passage he marks in the case of comparison that very effect of confluence that we have been stressing:

> "But if the plain truth be admitted that the *pure* idea of 'n' is never in the mind at all, when 'm' has once gone before; and that the feeling 'n-different-from-m' is itself an absolutely unique pulse of thought, the bottom of this precious quarrel drops out and neither party is left with anything to fight about." [1]

The use of the term "feeling" in this passage is unfortunate, but with the present conflict of psychological opinions there is no term that would be unexceptionable. "experience" is perhaps to be preferred. It marks the immediacy, and its generality is no drawback in the present state of our knowledge.

Analysis, synthesis, and all the rest of the logician's legitimate stock-in-trade tend to be treated in the same way as comparison by the psychologist. He describes them as if they were so many specific psychological processes. He may even tell his reader all about the syllogism, and methods of induction, saying at the end that no one thinks in syllogisms, or according to the logical methods of induction. They do not, any more than trees grow by the foot rule with which their growth may be measured. To discuss syllogisms when the topic is "thinking" is as misleading as to discuss foot rules when the topic is "trees."

If we give up the idea that there are special psychological abilities, some of which are possessed by some animals, some by others, we can conceive of a continuous evolution of mind which fits the facts as they are known. The stages in the evolution cannot be associated with the emergence of definite species. The differences of ability amongst individuals belonging to the same species are often as great

[1] James, *Principles of Psychology*, Vol. 1, p. 500. See also the note on the same page.

as the differences between species. In the simplest forms of animal behaviour, lack of sensory discrimination, together with a very limited repertory of movements results in behaviour which approximates to pure trial and error. If this limit is ever reached (a matter which has not been adequately tested), then confluence plays no part in determining the behaviour of that animal. At some stage the immediately past begins to influence the animal's behaviour in the present, e.g. he does not repeat a movement because a moment ago such movement exposed him to a painful stimulus. From this point onwards the evolution of behaviour takes the form of a progressive increase of the number of influences that work together to bring about the solution of the animal's problem. The more remote past begins to function, and then different experiences from the past play upon the same moment in the present. With increasing discrimination, different elements of the present play their part in shaping the solution. Finally, in the most intelligent actions, the adjustment and adaptation is the result of manifold influences weaving a highly specialized solution to the problem in mind.

The term evolution is so constantly and so firmly associated with the idea of a struggle and of striving, that an objector is almost sure to raise the question as to why the animal has problems that require new configurations for their solution. He may say, for instance, that by starting from the stage when the animal has his problem, we are leaving out the crucial factor in the evolution of mind. This is not denied. Intelligence is only a problem-solving organization. We have tried to understand it in terms of known facts and to envisage its development, but if there were not something more fundamental in mind no such organization would be needed. The point may be illustrated from a sentence that occurs in Prof. Elliot Smith's *Evolution of Man*:

"The high specialization of the sense of sight awakened in the creature (Tarsius) the curiosity to examine the objects around it with closer minuteness, and supplied guidance to the hands in executing more precise and more skilled movements than any that the Tree Shrew attempts." [1]

The " curiosity " is in one way the crux of the problem and even the apparently innocent statement that curiosity is aroused by keener vision masks one of the most fundamental problems in psychology. With our present knowledge, we can form no just conception of the drive that has led to the facing of new problems. We can, however, see that, given the drive, the organization of intelligence will play its part in formulating in detail the problem as well as in configuring the solution.

The Nature of Special Abilities

The contention that special abilities are not determined by differences in mental process is supported by the fact that the special abilities that have been found experimentally vary with every form and differentiation of the concrete material with which the individual is concerned. Dr. Burt shows this very clearly in *The Distribution of Educational Abilities*, in which the following diagram is given to illustrate the way in which various abilities seem to be related.[2]

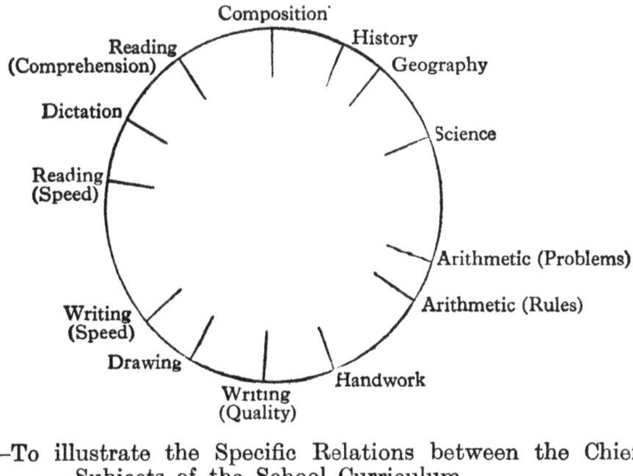

Fig. 7.—To illustrate the Specific Relations between the Chief Subjects of the School Curriculum.

[1] Op. cit., p. 32. [2] P. 59.

Each of the subjects round the circle has a specific element, but subjects near to one another are more alike in the special ability involved than are those far apart. Can we interpret these relations as due to the nature of the material involved? It seems that we can. For instance, the child's performance in writing (speed), dictation, reading, composition, history, geography, and even science, will be affected by his interest in, and mastery of, words. Other similarities and partial identities of material will affect subjects near to one another in this group. Towards the science end of the group special interests will count and in science itself the manipulation of numbers is likely to be involved as well as some reference to space relations. Towards the writing end of the group, muscular co-ordination will begin to be of importance. From writing (speed) to handwork, the importance of muscular co-ordination increases and the material with which each subject deals is specific. Arithmetic (rules) and arithmetic (problems) have a distinct element in common as far as their material is concerned. Finally, with regard to the relation of handwork to arithmetic and of science to arithmetic, it is obvious that they are likely to involve the same material to some degree.

Dr. Burt was dealing with a range of widely differing activities, but the same differentiation according to very slight changes in material have been found. Thus Prof. Muscio found that manual ability embraces as many special abilities as there are forms of material.[1] Miss McFarlane has found the same. The performance of her subjects varied not only with the material involved in the test, but even, to a lesser degree, with the object to be made.[2]

It is customary to think of a man who has marked special ability as having had it even when he lay in his cradle. We incline to think of it waiting ready to get busy upon its appropriate material. It is the view implied

[1] *British Journal of Psychology*, Vol. 13, 1922.

[2] *Ibid.*, Mon. Sup. A study of Practical Ability, 1925.

by Mr. Crummles when he is expecting an addition to his family:

"The talent of the other three is principally in combat and serious pantomime. I should like this one to have a turn for juvenile tragedy, I understand they want something of that sort in America very much. Perhaps it may have a genius for the tight rope."

From the scientific point of view it is impossible to think of special abilities as innate in this way. As we have seen, all the special abilities that come to light in experimental inquiries are specific to the material. It would be as absurd to say that a man is born with special abilities for these activities as that he is born with a special organ for taking snuff. This view which we have supported from the results of experimental psychology is adopted on quite other grounds by so eminent a biologist and anthropologist as Prof. Elliot Smith. He says:

"It would ill become me as a biologist to attempt to minimize the vast rôle played by heredity in determining the physical structure and the mental and moral aptitudes of every individual, and the variation in the average levels of attainment to which these hereditary qualities are subject in different races. But it is necessary to emphasize the fact that, so far as innate mental and moral characteristics are concerned, it is merely a vaguely defined and more or less generalized aptitude that is inherited, and not any special kind of ability or congenital propensity towards good or evil behaviour" (p. 66). ". . . the direction in which these aptitudes find expression is determined by the individual's personal experience and by his environment." [1]

Dr. Kate Gordon has shown that even when environmental influences are cancelled out, twins and siblings tend to resemble one another in degree of intelligence to an extent that convinces one of the importance of heredity for intelligence. This is in agreement with the results of testing and the constancy of the intelligence quotient in the individual. When more information with regard to special abilities has been accumulated, it may be possible to repeat Dr. Gordon's work, testing for special abilities

[1] Elliot Smith, *The Evolution of Man*, p. 116.

instead of general capacity. If from such work it should appear that siblings who have been brought up in different environments tend to have a considerable degree of correlation between their special abilities, then, and then only, would there be ground for maintaining that special abilities are innate.

CHAPTER VI

SPECIAL ABILITIES (*continued*)

THE PSYCHOLOGICAL FACTORS WHICH DETERMINE THE DEVELOPMENT OF SPECIAL ABILITIES

A CONSIDERATION of the results of tests of ability, and of other relevant facts has led to the conclusion that special abilities are complex, and it has favoured the presumption that their development depends upon a variety of psychological conditions. This view is put forward in Appendix 9 of the *Board of Education Report* by Mr. C. A. Richardson, H.M.I of Schools:

"Mr. Richardson thought it unlikely that special abilities existed in the same sense as general ability. It was becoming sufficiently evident that in all forms of 'intelligent' mental activity there was present a certain factor to which the name general ability might fairly be given. It then seemed probable that special ability or (better) aptitude, was a combination of general ability and special interest, and in some cases, special temperamental and physical characteristics."

The psychological activity manifested in all forms of ability is nothing but a series of intelligent acts such as we have described, and is therefore dependent on degree of confluence. This is the general factor which runs through all forms of ability. But the degree to which confluence is possible in relation to any given subject matter is dependent upon the individual's past experience (in this are included his interests) as well as upon his innate constitution. Given an individual in whom the general factor is present in a high degree, he will do well in all activities towards which he has any drive and for which he has acquired the relevant experiences. If, with regard to strength of drive and number of relevant experiences, he could be exactly matched with a person possessing a much lower degree of the general factor, he would always surpass him.[1] If, however, the individual of lower intelligence has a very strong drive towards any given activity and accumulates experience with regard to it, he may within this narrow sphere surpass the individual of much higher intelligence. An extreme instance of this has already been given in the case of the "genius" of Earlswood (p. 3). It is, of course, understood that this man in whom general capacity was so lacking, was only a genius as compared with other inmates of asylums for mentally defectives. There are a large number of the normal population who have ability far beyond his, even along the line of his speciality.

It will doubtless be objected to our view that on it there is no way of accounting for the fact that some people acquire special abilities much more easily than others who seem equally intelligent. Such an objection overlooks a number of psychological facts that are of first-rate importance. These facts may be divided into two groups, although in reality they are very intimately related:

1. Factors determining drive.
2. Factors determining the degree of confluence possible within a given field of activity.

1. Factors Determining Drive.—We have throughout assumed the factor of drive as essential to all forms of activity. In the present state of our knowledge it is quite impossible to show in detail how the degree of drive towards one activity differs from that towards another, although it is common knowledge that it does. It may be that the differentiation comes from the varying strength

[1] It should be noted that some years before the problem of general ability had been investigated by means of experimental methods, Prof. Stout expressed this view. See *Analytic Psychology*, Vol. 2, p. 34.

of instinctive drives in the individual. It cannot, however, be proved that there are innate differences in the strength of instinctive tendencies. Even if there are such differences, it is difficult to see how they determine such specific differences as appear in abilities. For instance, a man has the instinct of curiosity to a high degree ; will he be an astronomer, a bacteriologist, or merely an eavesdropper ? A more verifiable and certain cause of the differentiation in drive lies in the emotional and instinctive setting of the individual's early experiences in regard to any given subject matter. Let this setting be favourable, and he will tend to pursue his activities in relation to the particular subject matter : let it be unfavourable, and the field will become a limbo of impenetrable gloom through which he avoids making any unnecessary journeys. Throughout life affective experiences tell on the activities and the abilities of the individual, but there can be no doubt that it is the early ones that are the most potent in creating the illusion of innate special abilities.

2. Factors Determining Degree of Confluence possible within a given Field of Activity.—Under this heading there are two groups of influences of outstanding importance ; the one is related to experiences during the main developmental periods, the other to emotional ties.

A. The effect of experience during the main developmental periods.

The importance of experience during the developmental periods may be illustrated from the sphere of language. There is evidence that the formative period for language is the first three or four years of life. It is probable that even the crying and crowing of the first few months play their part in the development. Suppose that from illness the child is particularly lethargic during a part or the whole of this period ; suppose that he is punished for ceaseless babbling ; suppose that when he is at the imitative stage, either through deafness or the absence of models who use language well, he hears very little, is it likely that he will ever show special ability in activities which turn on the use of language? In his account of the linguistic activity of one day, Waddle quotes the instance of a child of three who used on an average 950 words per hour. The same considerations apply to the development of ability in all the different forms of concrete material. At some period every child tends to take an interest in numbers. Just as the corresponding tendency in language may not lead to natural fruition, so in number. The degree to which a variety of relevant and confluent experiences is essential may be illustrated from the incident quoted by Stern of a child of four, who when asked how many fingers his grandfather had, replied that he did not know, as he could only count his own.

It is probable that the tendency to "work over" the particular material ceaselessly at these developmental periods lays the foundation of a mastery that it is almost impossible to gain in later life. Long before the scientific study of ability, J. S. Mill, writing of his own education, says:

> ". . . . it may be useful that there should be some record of an education which was unusual and remarkable and which, whatever else it may have done, has proved how much more than is commonly supposed may be taught, and well taught, in those early years which, in the common modes of what is called instruction, are little better than wasted." [1]

In this he implies the importance of giving in the earliest years the experiences which are essential to the exercise of ability at a later stage. In the following passage he implies the converse of this theory, namely, that it is impossible to compensate for experiences which have been missed in the early years:

> "But as I had no boy companions, and the animal need of physical activity was satisfied by walking, my amusements, which were mostly solitary, were in general, of a quiet, if not a bookish turn, and gave little stimulus to any other kind of even mental activity than that which was already called forth by my studies: I conse-

[1] Mill, *Autobiography*, p. 1.

quently remained long, and in less degree have always remained, inexpert in anything requiring manual dexterity; my mind as well as my hands did its work very lamely when it was applied to the practical details which, as they are the chief interest in life to the majority of men, are also the things in which whatever mental capacity they have, chiefly shows itself." [1]

In order that we may test our theory of the importance for special abilities of experience during the main developmental periods, it becomes necessary to make a digression and to consider the subject of genius. In doing this we are assuming that genius is merely a marked degree of something that is possessed in varying degrees by all men. Modern scientific opinion seems to be inclined to this view.[2] Even if the relation between genius and insanity is absolutely established in the future, it need not be in opposition to this view. The most perfectly made, and the most finely adjusted, machinery is the most likely to be thrown out of gear. We do not, on this account, think of mechanical perfection and liability to go out of order, as two qualities having some occult connection. We recognize that the quality that ensures the one is liable, under certain conditions, to bring about the other. If the theory of ability that we have suggested is valid, we should expect to find that the genius is at least not lacking in general capacity, for genius lies in organizing what has remained discrete for the ordinary man. We should expect too, that in the early life of the genius influences favoured the development of the given form of special ability. Our study can only be suggestive. Even if sufficient evidence were available, it could not be brought within the limits of this treatment. We shall consider instances of some typical forms of genius including the artistic, but with regard to the latter it is obvious that the temperamental and even the physical characteristics of

[1] *Ibid.*, p. 21.

[2] See Terman, "New Approach to a Study of Genius," *Psychological Review*, 1922, and for an extensive bibliography of the subject, see Terman and Chase, "Psychology, Biology and Pedagogy of Genius," *Psychological Bulletin*, 1920.

which Mr. Richardson speaks (see p. 55), are likely to be particularly important. It may be that early experiences of the right kind, in addition to giving mastery over the material, favour the development of the attitudes, emotional and sensational, that are essential for artistic development. This cannot, of course, be proved, but it seems very likely when one considers such facts as that some music can grip the dog's organism in a veritable spasm, that many young children are moved to tears by music (Chopin was one of these), that modern writers on æsthetics speak with increasing unanimity of "systems of dispositions and tendencies orientated toward æsthetic experience." A violin does not give forth its finest tone until it has vibrated to sound for many years; it is at least likely that the human being cannot make fine music until he has similarly vibrated to it and there seems no doubt that the golden age for such vibration is during the very early years. The emotional renaissance that comes in the teens may afford another opportunity of awakening as far as appreciation is concerned, but it is probable that too much time will have been lost for such a late awakening to lead to the development of genius in music. The same considerations apply to all forms of art, although less obviously to literary production. This apparent exception fits in perfectly with our theory, for literary production is a field in which no one can well escape the relevant experience, or avoid gaining some degree of mastery of the essential elements at an early age, although the ability cannot develop fully for a long time.

Let us now turn to a study of the early years of some representative geniuses. Unfortunately, the details with regard to the early years—and the first four years are of great importance in this connection—are meagre. It is usual to regard ability in music as a special gift, and families in which it appears in two or three successive generations are quoted in confirmation of this view. But this is where the problem becomes complicated. Is the child of musical parents musical because he has inherited a special ability, or because he has had the necessary experiences in early years? A study of a number of cases shows that children without favourable heredity (as far as one can judge), have developed marked special ability when they have had appropriate experiences in the early period, and it is obvious that the children of parents with marked musical ability are much more likely to have the appropriate experience than are the children of "unmusical" parents. Handel and Mozart are an interesting pair in this respect. Mozart came of a musical family, Handel of a family that showed no musical ability, but they both gained musical experience and developed musical interests during the earliest years. Mozart was having lessons on the harpsichord at three years of age. Handel was taken to church in Halle and heard one of the finest organs of the period daily. In spite of his father's dislike of music, Handel had the opportunity of practising on a clavichord. Chopin's family was not particularly musical, but his father and several other members of the family were exceptionally intelligent. When he was very young he was so sensitive to music that he wept, though not painfully, whenever he heard it. His parents procured instruction for him while he was still very young. Many children show this early sensitiveness which seems to be a very close analogue of the dog's. In most families it is regarded as an unfortunate eccentricity and the individual learns to suppress it long before musical training has begun. It seems at least possible that, if training were commenced while this sensitiveness predisposes the child to interest in music, there might be more musical geniuses.

In *The Psychology of a Musical Prodigy* Révész expresses the opinion that musical ability is hereditary, and he implies a theory of musical faculties. The prodigy of whom he writes, Erwin Nyirigyhazi, was the son of a singer in opera choruses. Before the child was a year old he imitated song rather than speech. At the age of three his father had noted that he had an absolute ear for music. Both these facts show that the child had ample musical experiences in his early years, for even if such feats turned on the possession of a special ability it could not develop in this way without the experiences. Révész expresses the opinion that general ability is not important for the musical genius, but he reports that Erwin was about three years ahead of his years on tests. Thus, although Révész takes the opposite view from the one here put forward, his facts are not in conflict with it.

It is notable that musical genius comes to fruition at a very early age. This is always made a source of great wonder in literature, and yet it rests on a very simple consideration, namely, that the material and experiences essential for the development of musical ability are accessible to very young children. However great the ability of a child of four, he could not write a novel as he might write a musical composition, because the material is more complex, and involves a much greater degree of complexity in his relations with his environment. Stanley Hall and others have shown that different forms of genius develop at different ages. Presumably the age at which any form of genius develops is merely a measure of the number and complexity of the experiences upon which it depends ; some forms cannot develop until after experience has been enriched by the changes of the adolescent period, although they may depend upon favourable circumstances in the earlier period also.

When we turn from music to the arts of sculpture and painting, the development of the special ability is easier to trace because it does not come to fruition as early. Michelangelo stands out as one in whom the genius for both sculpture and painting was almost miraculous. In his case most biographers remark the lack of any sign of a similar gift in ancestors, or in his immediate relations. He was brought up by a foster nurse who was the wife of a stone-cutter and the daughter of a stone-cutter. Michelangelo says of himself :

"If I have anything good in my disposition it comes from my being born in the subtle air of your (Giorgio Vasari's) district of

Arezzo, just as also I drew in with the milk of my balia the chisels and the mallet that I make my figures with."

His childhood was spent amongst stone-cutters in the Settignano district and there can be no doubt that long before the age of thirteen he had gained experience of the shaping of stone. At that age he declared his determination to become a sculptor and his father conceded to his wish in spite of strong personal prejudice against such a career. It is well known that although he himself preferred the art of sculpture he was almost equally great as a painter. In the case of such a man it seems almost absurd to insist on the fact that he had unusual general capacity, it is so obvious, but the following passage is quoted because it illustrates the fact very well.

"There is perhaps no better comment on the many-sided powers of this great man than to recall the fact that three commissions which fell to him consecutively were of the following character—the first, to execute a group in sculpture of Samson and the Philistines; the second to construct the fortifications of San Miniato; and the third to prepare a design for an altar piece." [1]

He was very fond of reading, and although he left school at the age of thirteen, he had acquired a very fair education.

In Corot we have an example of a very different type of artistic genius. At first sight it would seem that any special hereditary gift was as much lacking in his case as in that of Michelangelo. His parents conducted a *magasin de modes.* His father kept the books and his mother made the dresses and millinery. Of his mother we are told "il n'y a qu'elle pour chiffoner de la sorte," in a fashion journal of the day. Thus it may be that Corot inherited from his mother those temperamental and physical characteristics that favour the development of artistic ability. As a child he lived away from home and we hear nothing of his early childhood. When he was eleven years of age he went to a school in Rouen. Living in this town

[1] Quoted by G. S. Davies, *Michelangelo,* 1924.

was a friend of the family, with whom he used to go for long walks:

"On s'asseyait au bord d'une rive tranquille et l'on assistait, dans le silence, au déclin de la lumière et à la fin du jour. Corot aimait à évoquer le souvenir des impressions ressorties alors par son âme d'enfant. Le charme des solitudes, le mystère des heures crépusculaires avaient dès ce temps-là fait éclore dans son jeune cœur la petite fleur de la poésie qui s'y épanouit plus tard et rayonna d'un si bel éclat."

At the age of nineteen he entered a drapery business, but neither here nor elsewhere did he show any interest in shop-keeping. At the age of twenty-six he gained freedom to pursue his art. His earlier work had little distinction, and it was not until the age of forty-four that his real genius began to show itself. There is nothing to show that Corot had outstanding general capacity, although from the way in which he managed his affairs when he became famous and wealthy, we may conclude that he was in no way lacking. His was an art that turned primarily on delicacy of feeling; through great labour that feeling came at last to triumphant expression, but it is significant that the lack of marked general capacity goes with late fruition and a very specialized form of genius.

As representing a form of art very different from the others that have been treated we may take Hogarth. His father was an unsuccessful schoolmaster and writer and there is no history of talent in the family, although a paternal uncle is said to have had a vein of satirical humour somewhat similar to the artist's. Hogarth says of himself:

"As I had naturally a good eye, and a fondness for drawing, shows of all sorts gave me uncommon pleasure when an infant and mimicry, common to all children, was remarkable in me. An early access to a neighbouring painter drew my attention from play; and I was at every possible opportunity employed in making drawings."

While these early tendencies and opportunities led to Hogarth's following art as a profession, his genius did not show itself until comparatively late. One of his biographers says:

"From 1723–30 he was employed upon designs and plates for a variety of publications. . . . None of these performances are at all superior to the common book embellishments of that period."

Hogarth was thirty-three in 1730. In 1731 his real genius was shown in *The Harlot's Progress*, which was the first of a long series of masterpieces. Hogarth's life is so very largely a history of his artistic productions that it is very difficult to obtain a clue to his ability for other activities. His pictures show, however, that he was a man of reflection, and his book on *The Analysis of Beauty* has many indications of his shrewdness, although it is marred by poverty of style and illiteracy.

These examples of artistic genius were chosen at random and without any definite prior knowledge of the childhood or parentage of the artists. It seems fair to claim that the details that are available favour the view that genius in art does not rest on the inheritance of a special ability, but on the possession of general capacity in proportion to the greatness of the art, together with some determining experiences in early childhood. Let us turn now to examples of genius in science.

As examples of very different forms of ability in science we may take Newton, Helmholtz, and Cuvier. From the following story it would seem that Newton had good general ability. The story is, that for some time he had been at the bottom of his class through inattention to his lessons. One day the top boy kicked him. As a revenge Newton determined to oust him from his position. This he did quite easily and remained top of his class. During his early years he made several mechanical toys and models. His biographer says: "Let it be remembered that we are not told that Newton when young took greatly to anything with the exception of the arts of construction." [1] Thus we have the case of a child with considerable general

[1] A. De Morgan, *Essays on the Life of Newton.*

capacity, gaining exceptional familiarity with spatial relations and the conditions of mechanical motion. Was he not very naturally the father of the man who discovered the laws of motion and the principle of gravitation? It is a pity that the rigour of modern historical criticism is throwing doubt on all such stories as that of Newton and the apple because it illustrates very beautifully the importance of confluence for the moment of genius. Just as in the case of the chimpanzee, quoted on p. 32, the functional value of a stick was carried over to an utterly different visual object, namely a blanket, so the functional value of the falling apple was carried over to apparently stationary worlds. It is interesting to note that Prof. Stout in describing this act of intelligence uses the term confluence. He says:

> "Thus the discovery of gravitation took place through a confluence of the mental system representing what was known of terrestrial gravity and the system representing what was known of the motion of the heavenly bodies." [1]

Cuvier was the son of a soldier. His mother seems to have been a very capable woman and there can be no doubt that in teaching him to draw, and in supervising his home-work, she contributed to his later success. He showed no special interests until at the age of ten he came across a book on natural history written by Gesner. This he devoured and spent hours copying the pictures, using silks for colouring when his supply of paints ran out. Later, he used Buffon's monumental work in the same way. He did well in all his school subjects and in his first year at the university won high distinctions in language and literature. Owing to adverse circumstances he was prevented, first from qualifying for the Church, and later, for political life. As a consequence, he went as tutor in a family living on the coast of Normandy. Here he made that first-hand study of molluscs that had such an important influence upon the rest of his work, and which

[1] Stout, *Analytic Psychology*, Vol. 2, p. 111.

finally committed him to scientific research. His progress and his brilliance in this work are so well known that they need not be recounted here. Cuvier makes a very interesting contrast with Newton. As Newton was the foremost physicist of his day, so was Cuvier the foremost comparative anatomist of his, but the latter never achieved a mental act that could be compared with Newton's formulation of the theory of gravitation. Cuvier affords an illustration of how the accumulation of knowledge through very persevering study may lead to valuable results even though the person who accumulates it is not capable of the very high degree of confluence essential for the brilliant generalizations that have led to the greatest advances in science. While Cuvier was certainly a very capable man (this is shown by his plans for national education, and his other activities outside the field of his main interest), there can be little doubt that his innate intelligence was considerably lower than Newton's. Correspondingly, we find that many of his generalizations proved false, and that he failed to make the great generalization for which his knowledge pre-eminently fitted him. This view seems justified even when allowance has been made for the great complexity of the subject-matter with which he had to deal.

In Helmholtz the highest qualities of both Newton and Cuvier met. He was indefatigable in study and the collection of facts, he showed extraordinary brilliance in the formulation of hypotheses.[1] Helmholtz' father was a schoolmaster of considerable learning: "At home he occupied himself in arousing his children . . . to a sense of the ideal in poetry, art, and music." Judging from his school reports, Helmholtz had good general capacity. For German, Latin, Greek, Hebrew, Religious Instruction, Mathematics and Physics, he was marked "good"; for

[1] This sentence is not meant to imply that Newton neglected facts, but simply that circumstances did not necessitate for him such intensive and many-sided research as they did both for Cuvier and Helmholtz.

History and Geography, "excellent." The circumstances determining his interests are very well shown in the following passages from his *Autobiography* :

"From the time of my childish playing with wooden blocks, the relations of spatial proportion to each other were well known to me from actual perception. What sort of figures were produced when bodies of regular shape were laid against each other, I knew well without much consideration. When I began the scientific study of geometry, all the facts which I had to learn were perfectly well known and familiar to me, much to the astonishment of my teachers. . . ." (p. 271).

"As I became bigger and stronger I went about with my father and my schoolfellows a great deal in the neighbourhood of my native town, Potsdam, and I acquired a great love of nature. This is perhaps the reason why the first fragment of physics which I learned in the Gymnasium engrossed me much more closely than purely geometrical and algebraical studies."[1]

When he was leaving school he asked his father to be allowed to become a physicist. His father explained that this was impossible from the financial point of view unless he became an army surgeon, and so obtained the training which was given by the State. Helmholtz agreed to this, and thus this man of outstanding ability, in physics and mathematics, gained also a knowledge of the facts of physiology and of the other biological sciences. Here again his own views are interesting :

"I must say that I ascribed my success in great measure to the circumstances that, possessing some geometrical capacity and equipped with a knowledge of physics, I had by good fortune been thrown among medical men, where I found a virgin soil of great fertility ; while, on the other hand, I was led by the consideration of vital processes to questions and points of view which are usually foreign to mathematicians and physicists."

If there had been no mind in which all these different aspects of nature came together under conditions favouring confluence, it seems highly probable that a large number of the most promising theories of modern science would not have been formulated.

[1] Helmholtz, *Autobiography*. Popular Science Lectures, Vol. 2.

In his study of great calculators,[1] Binet gives very valuable information with regard to an ability which, perhaps more than any other, has been regarded as simple and innate. He summarizes the circumstances common to the great calculators whom he has studied. They are:

1. Lack of hereditary influences that would account for the special ability.
2. The same lack with regard to environmental influences.
3. Birth in a miserable milieu.
4. Great precocity in the development of the special ability.
5. Illiteracy.
6. Complete absorption of interest in figures.
7. Dependence of the ability upon exercise.

Birth in a miserable *milieu* seems, at first sight, as though it must be an irrelevant coincidence, but consideration of what it means from the psychological side suggests that it may be the most important determining factor. A miserable *milieu* results in the child having few distractions; any activity that he can carry on in such an environment is likely to be practised to an enormous degree. Most of the great calculators have developed their ability before they learned to read or write. This means that at the time when they began to calculate, it was the one activity open to them. It may even be that their very poverty gave to numeration a special fascination because of its association with wealth. However this may be, calculation took for them the place of games and phantasy. The majority of the calculators of whom Binet speaks were ignorant and narrow in their interests, although as a class they were by no means lacking in intelligence. In strong contrast to them stands

[1] For discussion of the question as to whether great calculators should be classed with geniuses, see below, p. 70.

Rückle, a great calculator whom Müller studied.[1] Rückle was a well-educated man of exceptional ability in both languages and mathematics. In the simple operations of the four rules he was slower than Inaudi who was certainly his inferior in general intelligence and education. In more difficult problems, however, Rückle excelled. Müller gives as the explanation of this that while Inaudi had spent his days working over the simpler rules in a way that would have irked a man of wider interests, Rückle had spent his time in dealing with the higher problems in which he became familiar with those characteristics of numbers that made the solution of the more difficult problems easy for him.

It is significant for our theory that these exceptionally gifted calculators lost their ability when they ceased to practise for a time, and that Ampère and Gauss, who were prodigies at calculating when they were young, lost the greater part of their ability when they became mathematicians and their interests accordingly widened. Binet thinks it strange that facility in the abstract should develop at the early age it does in the great calculator. But surely, it is its very abstraction that makes such early development possible! Let the child once master the idea of the number system, and he can carry on his calculations without any further concrete experience. It may very well be that it is this abstract nature that repels so many children, whose environment presents them with more alluring activities.

The question has been raised as to whether great calculators should be classed with geniuses. Presumably, Prof. Ward would be inclined to answer the question in the negative.[2] It may be granted that their productions differ from the other productions of genius in that they can be checked by a number of mechanical devices, e.g. calculating machines, whereas it is usual to stress the

[1] Müller, "Zur Analyse der Gedachtnistätigkeit," u.s.w., *Zeitschrift für Psychologie*, Ergänzungsband 5 .

[2] Ward, *Principles of Psychology*, pp. 450–1.

creativeness, the incalculability of genius. As far as the production is concerned this difference is important. From the point of view of the psychological process involved it is difficult to see that there is a valid distinction. A Newton, in order to solve his problem, gains exceptional familiarity with the material involved. His success depends on the degree to which all the conditioning factors and the relevant connections can come together to shape the solution. The same is true of the great calculator and each solution is a " creation " (the size and variety of the numbers preclude the possibility of the solutions being known from memory).

Further discussion of the subject of genius will take us no further on our road. This brief survey will have served its purpose if it does no more than suggest to those who incline to a belief in innate special abilities, the plausibility of Dr. Johnson's statement in the *Life of Cowley*, " The true genius is a man of large general power(s), accidentally determined to some particular direction."

B. Emotional Ties

We have already noted the importance of emotion as a drive towards or away from a given activity. In this section we are to consider its effect on confluence in the field of any given subject-matter. It is a commonplace of psychology that emotional experience strengthens the associative bonds between all the elements connected with the experience. It is equally a commonplace that the association of factors in incongruent emotional complexes inhibits their association with one another. Thus emotion has a very important effect upon confluence.[1] Its influence on intelligence as measured by tests is put very emphatically by Dr. Burt in the following passage :

[1] The objector may say that therefore emotion is another factor in intelligence. Reflection will show, however, that this would be as absurd as to say that the wind is part of the horsepower of a locomotive.

"'Every psychological test,' it has been said, 'is inevitably a test of intelligence.' Too often it is forgotten that every test of intelligence is also a test of emotion. A neglect of the emotional aspect of an examination of intelligence may send many a normal child to the special school as mentally deficient. No matter how scrupulously uniform the procedure, how sympathetic the examiner's tone, the child's excitability will introduce disturbances in unknown quantity. To appeal constantly to the invigorating emotions—to pleasure, curiosity, pride, self-display, sociability, confidence; and to banish utterly the depressing emotions—anxiety, fear, grief, disgust, shyness, self-suppression, sense of failure, these are the soundest rules." [1]

Just as these emotions may influence the subject's performance on a test of general ability, so they may enter into dispositions permanently connected with some special activity and determine the individual's degree of ability in that activity.

The Psycho-Analysts have emphasized the effect of suppressed or repressed emotion upon the individual's ability in any given subject-matter. Dr. Rivers says:

"The knowledge derived from psycho-analysis goes to show that this suppressed early experience may have a great effect on character and may play an important part in determining likes and dislikes and tendencies to special lines of activity in later life." [2]

Dr. Ernest Jones quotes the case of a man who suffered in this way in regard to mathematical ability. When the repression was removed his disability went also.[3]

It is obvious that on the theory that the general factor in intelligence is degree of confluence, the person of strong emotions is likely to appear unintelligent. His ideas are liable to be tied up in knots, as it were, so that confluence is constantly inhibited or narrowed. A most interesting illustration of this is afforded by Goethe's attack upon the Newtonian theory of light. His antagonism was aroused by Newton's theory of the composition of white light, on account of some æsthetic prejudice that he harboured.

[1] Burt, *Mental and Scholastic Tests*, p. 16.
[2] Rivers, *Instinct and the Unconscious*, p. 76.
[3] Jones, *Psycho-Analysis*, 3rd ed., p. 648.

Although he studied Newton's theory and experimented for himself he never came to understand the matter, but displayed a childish ignorance and lack of science. The rôle of emotion in producing this stupidity in one of the world's geniuses may be gauged from the fact that he called Newton's propositions "incredibly impudent," "mere twaddle," "admirable for children in a go-cart," "nothing but lying and plenty of it."

CHAPTER VII

SUMMARY AND CONCLUSIONS

THE view of Ability that has been suggested may be summarized in relation to the version of the Parable of the Talents in which one man received five talents, another two talents, and the third one talent. The number of talents which each man is originally given, corresponds on our theory to his degree of intelligence, i.e. the degree to which his experiences are confluent. As in the parable, so in the case of mental gifts, all are not equally endowed. The original endowment may be used in a number of ways. However it is used, it will lead to the development of special abilities. The drive to use it in one way or another comes from the person's emotional and instinctive nature in relation to the exigencies of the environment. The man who hid his talent in the earth suffered from fear and resentment, Dr. Burt's depressing emotions.[1] In some cases he suffers from a lack of any attractive venture in which to invest it, in others, from a mere lack of the invigorating emotions. The man who has many talents (i.e. good general capacity) seems almost sure to invest them, even if nothing better presents itself than the mere manipulation of numbers. While the facts seem to show that a man with good general capacity may, in unfavourable circumstances, develop only one narrow line of interest, the chances are in favour of his interests being broad. For the high degree of confluence not only leads to an efficient focusing of the whole of experience

[1] See above, p. 72.

upon the given problem, but also, in that very focusing, the relation of the problem of the moment to quite different aspects of experience is given, whereby those aspects may in turn become objects of interest. The case of Helmholtz, quoted on p. 68 above, is a good illustration of this.

The acceptance of this interpretation has certain practical consequences with regard to early education and with regard to testing ability. If the experiences of the first few years are as important for all later development as they seem to be, it is obvious that greater attention should be given to them. In the Nursery School Movement this is being recognized, but Nursery Schools affect only a small part of the population and only a few hours of the day for that part. Further, while much of the work that is done in Nursery Schools is admirable, the workers mostly lack the psychological knowledge and outlook that would be needed for our purpose. Before any system can adapt itself perfectly to the needs of the very young child, psychology must have undertaken an intensive study of a number of children from birth to four or five years of age, and have based upon this study suggestions for giving in the environment the possibility of developing all the different kinds of activity that are basic to all the most important special abilities. This does not mean that the child should be forced or given the kind of education that J. S. Mill received. It implies, on the contrary, that the hindrances which stand in the way of the full mental development of the average young child should be removed, and that all the tendencies towards achievement that he develops spontaneously should be given scope in an appropriate form.

The problem of the emotional setting at the early period is much more difficult. The general injunction to encourage the invigorating emotions will hold, but at this early stage the matter is extraordinarily delicate. A chance association, a fear coming from misunderstanding, may lead to the neglect of a whole field of experience and this may lay the foundation of a lasting inability in relation to that field.[1]

From the facts that have been considered in the preceding chapters, certain conclusions with regard to the practice of testing may be drawn. The subject may be discussed under three headings : tests of general capacity, tests in relation to education, and tests in relation to vocational selection and guidance.

Tests of General Capacity

Our conclusions with regard to the nature of intelligence bring us to the view which has been advanced so emphatically on statistical grounds by Prof. Spearman—the desirability of combining tests of a number of different activities. If this is done, chance variations in interest and in familiarity with different materials will tend to be compensated. In the past, tests of general capacity have been very largely verbal ; they have tested the candidate's ability to use words and other symbols. Herring in justifying this says :

> " Total human nature and the mutual demands of human beings have become such that intelligence, as it is required for success in contemporaneous human society, comprises largely the ability to deal effectively with situations involving the use of language and of mathematical and other symbols, both subjective and conventional, and also the ability to control situations through the analysis and interpretation of novel and complicated phenomena." [2]

No one would deny that the intelligent person will master the use of symbols in relation to his own fields of interest and activity, but these fields are very divergent, and we have already seen (p. 51) that very small divergencies in the field, affect the individual's performance to a marked degree. In Part II of this book we shall see that one of the best-authenticated tests of general capacity

[1] Cf. Watson, *Psychology from the Standpoint of a Behaviourist*, p. 212.

[2] Herring, " Verbal and Abstract Elements in Intelligence Examinations," *Journal of Educational Psychology*, Vol. 12, 1921.

is done better by those who specialize in language, than by those who specialize in science. Further, Miss Gaw has shown that children who do not shine in the linguistic tests may do well in performance tests.[1] As Herring claims, the exceptionally clever and successful are likely to be able to do well in tests involving language and other symbols, but if the examiner wishes to discriminate between two individuals who have average grades on such tests, he will find it valuable to supplement these with a variety of others. He may find that one of these " average people " scores well in a wide range of non-linguistic tests, while the other shows no better ability in these than in the linguistic tests. The former testee may be handicapped in the linguistic tests from some of the causes that we have enumerated, the latter may have had no specific handicap, but may possess only average general capacity.

Tests in Relation to Education

If a child who shows high general capacity in a psychological test shows no exceptional ability in his school work, the believers in innate special abilities may quite well take the attitude that this is not surprising, but simply means that he has no particularly strong special " engine." Such a view is not possible on the theory that we have suggested. A child who has high general ability and who shows no pre-eminence in any of the special abilities involved in school work, should be made the object of a careful study in order that a person of high potential efficiency may not be wasted. There are several possibilities :

(*a*) His interest may already have been diverted to activities which find no place in the curriculum, and his time in school may be spent in dreaming and in planning what he will do immediately he escapes (cf. Newton and Helmholtz).

(*b*) The school work may have no strong competitor

[1] Frances Gaw, " A Study of Performance Tests," *British Journal of Psychology*, Vol. 15.

for his attention, but may in itself be so deadly and so much beneath the range of his capacity that it never makes an appeal. Or the same result may come from unfavourable emotional attitudes to the master or his schoolfellows.

(*c*) From physical or temperamental causes there may be a lack of drive.

For (*a*) and (*b*) the remedy is obvious, and it lies along the line of progress that is being followed in education. For (*c*) our present knowledge does not help very much, but there is every hope that in the future the school clinic will be able to deal with such cases. Much that is known with regard to perversions and the development of bad habits of mind and body during the early period will bear on these cases and will again point to the necessity for expert treatment of the child during the first few years.

For children whose general ability falls below a certain standard, it may be desirable to prescribe a restricted curriculum, chosen as the result of careful study and experiment. It may be that some subjects involve a degree of confluence that is absolutely beyond their capacity. In all subjects it will take them longer to attain the degree of familiarity that favours confluence. It therefore seems essential that they should have longer for each subject, and attempt fewer, than the more able child.

The problem of testing for special abilities becomes very important towards the upper end of the school. But this subject may be treated under the next heading.

Vocational Selection and Guidance

These terms might seem to the uninitiated to stand for one and the same thing. That they do not signify two aspects of the same process is due largely to the nature of ability. Most industrial tasks can be performed by a man of good general ability, and each employer is naturally tempted to choose for his work the man who seems generally "bright." Such selection fails to serve the purpose of guidance as far as the worker is concerned for the following reasons:

(1) Although the "bright" man's good general capacity enables him to come up to a certain average performance, his lack of some previous special experience may prevent his doing as well as a man of less intelligence who has had that special experience.

(2) Even though he performs the given task very well, there may be other tasks for which he has developed special abilities and in which his labour would be much more valuable.

(3) The work may be so much below his capacity that it soon leads to boredom and undesirable emotional attitudes.

(4) By the selection of the more able man, the man of less general ability, who could perform this particular task and few others, is kept out of a job.

In the past, the competitive examinations for such work as that of the lower branches of the Civil Service have probably done more harm than any of the haphazard choosing of individual employers. The examinations, on account of their range and the keenness of the competition, tended to the selection of individuals of high general capacity. The work for which they were chosen could be done by a person of very average intelligence. The result was that in these branches there was an unusually large number of disappointed and unhappy workers who probably did their work less well than people of lower general ability who have developed the special and often very narrow ability required.

Before guidance and selection can be organized for the good of the worker, a very exhaustive series of investigations will have to be carried out. Jobs must be studied and tests for the special abilities involved in them, or norms for performance on the job itself, must be devised. Work should be classified according to the standard of general capacity essential for its performance. The degree of general capacity essential for the development of various special abilities should be studied. Most of these problems are already occupying research workers in different countries,[1] and there is no doubt that in time men will be chosen for their work as scientifically as a metal is chosen for the strain that it will bear. To some this will seem the end of romance, but there is probably little ground for fear on that score and, in any case, it is not the concern of science.

Part II of this book will deal with tests for the selection and guidance of university students. It will include an account of an experimental study recently carried out at Bedford College, the object of which was to find tests for the more important special abilities in the work of the Arts, and of the Science Faculties, respectively.

[1] In England such work is being done by the National Institute of Industrial Psychology. For an account of the work that is being done in other countries, see Stott, *Report on the Present Position of Vocational Guidance and Vocational Selection*, 1924.

PART II

TESTS FOR UNIVERSITY STUDENTS

CHAPTER I

TESTS FOR THE SELECTION OF UNIVERSITY STUDENTS

IN the case of university students the problems of selection and guidance are perhaps more distinct than they are for any other group of workers that has been tested. On account of the two facts, that the accommodation is limited, and that any one with ability below a certain minimum is not likely to benefit by a university education, selection becomes a very important problem. The university entrance examinations give a rough gauge of the information that the individual has acquired in a number of subjects, and this is to some considerable degree a real measure of his ability. The weakness of such examinations for the purposes of selection comes from two sources. In the first place, students of good ability who have had a poor schooling are at an unfair disadvantage ; in the second place, some schools develop a highly efficient cramming technique that enables them to foist upon the universities students who are not fitted to benefit by a university course. For these reasons it is desirable to have a psychological test of intelligence as an aid to selection. It does not seem desirable that this should take the place of the test of knowledge, but the two should be taken into account. All those who stand high in the test of knowledge may be accepted without question. All those who stand high on the test of intelligence may be accepted provided that they do not show such a lack of knowledge as would suggest slackness and a lack of the other " moral " qualities that are essential for success. In choosing candidates from amongst the remainder, who do not distinguish themselves in either the knowledge or the intelligence tests, the results of the two must be considered in conjunction—if there is little to choose between two candidates from the point of view of their results in the knowledge examination, the one who is better on the test of ability should be chosen.

In view of much that has been written with regard to the use of tests of intelligence in American colleges, this will seem a very conservative view of their use. It must be remembered, however, that the American system of education imposes a much less drastic selection of candidates before the university stage than the English system. On this account, differences in intelligence amongst those presenting themselves for college entrance there, are much more significant than they are here. But even allowing weight to this consideration it may be that the importance of general intelligence is at present being over-stressed in some of the American college entrance examinations, although in others the inclusion of a considerable number of general-information questions probably avoids this one-sidedness. It is interesting to note that Pintner, in his recently published book on Intelligence Testing,[1] emphasizes the comparatively low correlations between tests of intelligence and academic grades in American colleges in which the tests have been carried out. The Thorndike Test, which is the only one quoted by him that gives correlation coefficients above ·5, is very largely a test of general information on subjects that would count in the academic scores. The fact that, with groups as much selected as those who present themselves for college

[1] University of London Press, 1924.

entrance, the test of intelligence is not of great prognostic value, should emphasize the need for tests of the factors that are important in determining the success of the students in their college work. These factors must be qualities of character, and special abilities.

At Columbia University all the different aspects of the problem seem to have been solved to the satisfaction of the authorities. The students applying for admission form a comparatively heterogeneous group, so that the Thorndike Intelligence Test forms a very good means of grading them and deciding which of the candidates are not likely to benefit by a university education. In *Measurement in Higher Education*,[1] Wood gives an exceedingly interesting account of the results of the use of the Thorndike Test at Columbia and says that in future all students entering Columbia College for the first time will be required to submit to two examinations : (1) the intelligence examination, and (2) the content-placement examination. The content-placement examination " will consist of a battery of New Type objective tests for achievement in English, Mathematics, Modern Languages, Science and History. Every candidate will be required to take at least the following sections of this battery :

1. English.
2. Mathematics.
3. One Modern Language."

The inclusion of this test of knowledge shows that even where a very successful test of intelligence, lasting nearly three hours, is used, it is still recognized that the test of achievement is important. Its being called " New Type " marks the fact that it is standardized and that the majority of the answers may be marked mechanically. There are obvious advantages in using such an examination in order to obtain a preliminary survey of the students' knowledge of facts, but one reads with astonishment that this type of examination is now being used

[1] World Book Co., 1923.

throughout all subjects and all grades of work at Columbia. Thus for the mid-year examination in Philosophy the modern American Socrates is faced with this :

"The following statements are either true or false. If you think a statement true put a + (plus) sign in front of it; if false, put a – (minus) sign. If any part of the statement is false, the whole statement is considered false. If there are statements which you consider debatable put plus or minus as the argument for its truth or falseness seems to you better. Put a circle round such plus or minus, but around these only. Such debatable questions are not those in which any part is clearly false." (Then follows information as to marks to be gained.)

Sample statements :

"The quick decisions and ready attention of the impulsive man render him a steady and reliable leader into new and profitable fields."

"In some cases of reflection the probability and desirability of a predicted outcome furnish the reason for the decision reached."

"If the ultimately simple elements out of which material bodies are formed are alone real, then the real world is the world of molecules." [1]

There are three or four pages of such statements to be marked. Have the test enthusiasts at Columbia really converted their colleagues to the use of this kind of thing or have they merely hypnotized them temporarily? A little reflection might convince even New Type examiners that some inaccuracy in grading is to be preferred to creating the kind of attitude, and encouraging the type of mind, that would flourish under such a system.

Wood mentions the importance of character traits and moral habits for college success (p. 135). Apparently Columbia has not developed any separate tests for these qualities, but Wood implies that the very strenuousness of the atmosphere that has been created by the new

[1] Wood, op. cit., pp. 256–7.

scientific methods of grading, tends to act as a selective agent.

A Plea for the Study of Special Trends

It is to be hoped that along with the development of better methods of selecting university students by means of intelligence tests there will arise a study of individual trends. From what has been shown in Part I it is obvious that keen interest in and devotion to a subject from early years may give a mastery that enables the individual to achieve feats that are impossible for those who have not gained such experience. Tests of intelligence do not enable the psychologist to measure the difference between such an individual and one who has not developed any special field of interest. Both of these supposititious individuals may have average general intelligence, but the one who has already achieved is certainly more likely to benefit by a university course than the one who has not. It is probable that in view of the degree of selection that takes place before candidates present themselves for a college intelligence test, the differences of intelligence in those tested are practically unimportant as compared with differences that would be found in a less selected group. By this it is not meant that the most intelligent university student is not much more intelligent than the least. On the contrary, he certainly is. What is claimed, is that even the least intelligent university student is likely to have sufficient intelligence to do work that is worth while, provided that he wants to do it and has not had some serious special handicap. To the present writer it seems that very great harm may be done by over-emphasizing the importance of high general intelligence. There can be no doubt that any one who is not seriously below the average in intelligence may do very useful and even original work in subjects to which he is devoted, while the possessor of much higher intelligence, lacking such devotion, may achieve little. The man in the Rolls-

Royce may have an easier time and may get to his journey's end sooner than the man in a Ford, but he may not; and in any case, it is only on the very long and difficult journeys that the difference is of practical importance.

CHAPTER II

TESTS FOR THE GUIDANCE OF UNIVERSITY STUDENTS

An Account of an Attempt to find Tests for Special Abilities in the Work for Arts and Science Degrees

TESTS for the guidance of university students, with regard to the studies that they should pursue, have not been developed. The task of finding such tests is a difficult one on account of the complexity and variety of university work. The justification for attempting it is that university students are beyond the age at which they are likely to develop some of the most fundamental abilities.[1] If, therefore, they lack these to a marked degree it is advisable for them to avoid the subjects in which they are involved. The fundamental choice for most university students is between science and arts, and casual observation seems to suggest that there are special abilities involved in the work of each of these faculties; for instance, lack of manipulative skill is more likely to hinder a Science, than an Arts student. The present study was undertaken to gain statistical evidence on this question of the importance of special abilities in arts and science, respectively. It aimed at framing tests for the special abilities that are essential in the work of each of the faculties. In undertaking such a study the

[1] See above, Part I, p. 57 f.

experimenter made no assumptions as to the ultimate nature of arts and science subjects as such, nor as to their relation. There is no doubt that the subjects included in each faculty vary very much amongst themselves and that in many ways the distinction between arts and science is an artificial one. These considerations do not affect the practical problem. It is still possible that in arts the lack of certain abilities may not be as fatal as in science, and *vice versa*. A student cannot, of course, have too many special abilities for either faculty, but it is at least possible that he may lack a special ability that is essential in one of the faculties and not in the other.

If tests for the more important special abilities could be found, it was hoped that they might be used for purely advisory purposes, i.e. to warn students who would be likely to have special difficulties in either faculty. The present study was entirely exploratory and designed to test the possibility of such a scheme. It was not anticipated that the tests invented would all be satisfactory, or that they would cover the whole ground. It was recognized also, that even if satisfactory tests were found, further work on norms of performance would be necessary. The work is still in progress, but the results of the three years of testing now completed may be of interest. To the experimenter, while they point to the need of further modification of individual tests, they hold the promise of some measure of success.

That some form of guidance based on the study of the individual's abilities would be desirable is evident as soon as one considers how haphazard is the choice of faculty with most students. At school the boy or girl is obliged to study the subjects that parents or teachers prescribe, and in the case of an individual with a university career in view, the choice of subjects is further influenced by matriculation requirements. Throughout the school period it seems true that, on the whole, the subjects studied by an individual are not chosen with reference to the special abilities and interests that he has begun to develop. As it is essential that the child should acquire a fairly wide range of knowledge, this arbitrariness in his curriculum is probably inevitable and it gives him the opportunity of developing a number of special abilities. At the beginning of his university career the student is naturally influenced in his choice of subjects by his school experience, but the reduction in the number of subjects to be studied gives him an opportunity of dropping those for which he has a marked distaste or disability. To the student with a high degree of some special ability it gives the opportunity of beginning a course leading to a specialized study, which may lead on to a brilliant career. These possibilities should make the choice of subjects at the beginning of the university course a matter of careful consideration. Usually, however, the choice is very haphazard. The student is influenced largely by prejudices formed during his school life ; these together with the exigencies of time tables and other matters of university regulation usually determine his choice, both of faculty, and of the special subjects within the faculty.

The Choice of Tests

As the purpose of this study was to find out the factors leading to failure in either science or arts, a number of lecturers were asked to suggest the causes of students' failures in their respective subjects. In a number of cases the lack described was one that would come under the head of "general ability," in other cases the lack of moral qualities was described, but a certain number of special abilities were mentioned. Taking the evidence from all sources, it seemed desirable to devise tests which should involve each one of the following abilities :

For the Arts Faculty :

Rapidity of controlled verbal association.
Ability to recall.
Appreciation of style.[1]

[1] In 1921 tests for three other abilities were tried, but discarded for various reasons.

For the Science Faculty:

Ability to remember and to follow directions given verbally.

Ability to solve problems involving spatial relations.

Ability to classify, and to generalize with regard to, concrete objects.

Ability to grasp and express relations by means of symbols (other than words).

Two tests of general capacity, prose completion and analogies, were also given.

The time that was allowed for each test is given with the sample series of tests which follows. The tests in Book A were, on account of their nature, speed tests. For all the tests that occur in Book B, the time was so ample that this book cannot be regarded as a test of speed, the time was regulated merely to keep the conditions as uniform as possible. The series of tests that was used in 1923 is given below. The series for 1921 and 1922 were identical in form but different in material, apart from the fact that some tests were given in 1921 that were not repeated, and that the Memory Test was not given in 1921.

The following note was read to the candidates before they began the tests:

"The tests which you will have this morning are not designed to test your intelligence. They are planned to throw light on the relations between different kinds of ability and we ask you to submit to them in order that we may discover whether they answer this purpose or not. You will probably all find some of them difficult. The results would be of no use to us if you were able to do them with ease. If for any reason you cannot do a test, wait for the next. Do your best and do not worry about the results."

October, 1923.

A

Fill in the following and read what is printed below.

	Surname	Christian Names
Name in full:		

	Years	Months
Age:		

The tests to be written in this book will be timed. Work as rapidly as possible.

NEVER TURN A PAGE UNTIL YOU ARE TOLD.

TEST 1A. Time 3 mins.

(1) Copy the figure given below, but make all lines twice the length of the original lines.

(NOTE.—The paper for this test was squared.)

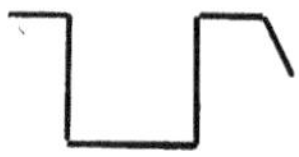

THIS SPACE IS FOR YOUR DRAWING.

(2) Copy the figure given below, but change its position on the paper, as the position of the figure in the example is changed.

EXAMPLE

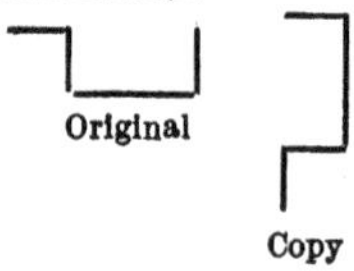

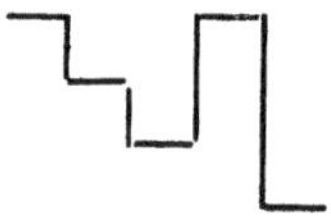

THIS SPACE IS FOR YOUR DRAWING.

(3) Copy the figure given below, doubling the length of the horizontal, and halving the length of the vertical lines.

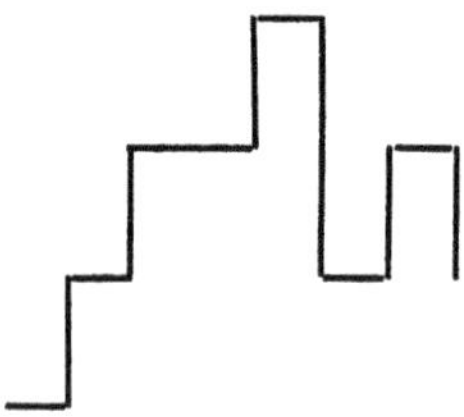

THIS SPACE IS FOR YOUR DRAWING.

Do not turn this page until you are told.

TEST 1B. Time 30 secs.

Trace a line showing how you would pass from S through the maze to E without crossing any line.

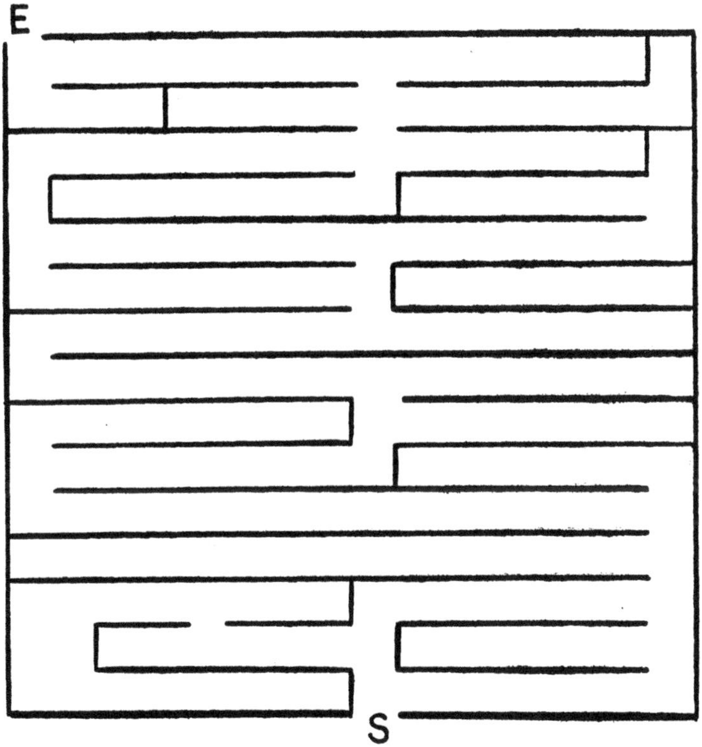

Do not turn this page until you are told.

TEST 1B—Continued. **Time 45 secs.**

Trace a line showing how you would pass from S through the maze to E without crossing any line.

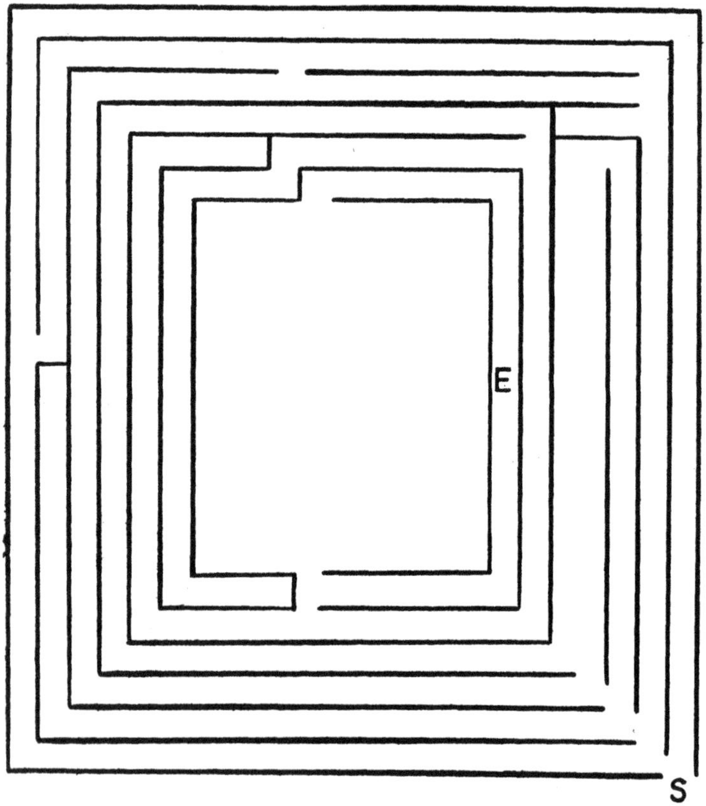

Do not turn this page until you are told.

<u>TEST 1B—Continued.</u> **Time 45 secs.**

Trace a line showing how you would pass from S through the maze to E without crossing any line.

Do not turn this page until you are told.

TEST 2. **2 mins.**

Write down as many different adjectives as you can.

Write down as many adverbs ending in "ly" as you can.

TEST 2—Continued. **2 mins.**

Write down as many adjectives descriptive of the sea as you can.

Write down as many three-syllabled words as you can.

TEST 3.

The following directions were read aloud to the students, who had to apply them in relation to the lines of print given on the next page.

"Turn to Test 3. In this test you will have to carry out instructions which will be given once only. The word 'attend' will precede the giving of each set of instructions.

"Attend. Do not look down. In line 4, if there are fewer than five vowels, put a comma after each consonant; if there are more than four vowels put a semi-colon after each digit. Pens up. Ready, go. (Allow 15 secs.) Pens down. Blot the page.

"Attend. Do not look down. In line 7, put a cross under every odd number and a circle round every multiple of four. Pens up. Ready, go. (Allow 15 secs.) Pens down. Blot the page.

"Attend. Do not look down. In line 1, cross out any letters which occur in the word 'armistice.' Pens up. Ready, go. (Allow 15 secs.) Pens down. Blot the page.

"Attend. Do not look down. In line 6, put the letter 'e' in all the triangles, the letter 'w' in all the quadrilaterals, and the letter 'h' in all the circles. Pens up. Ready, go. (Allow 15 secs.) Pens down. Blot the page.

"Attend. Do not look down. In line 2, turn every full-stop into a colon and put a circle round every exclamation mark. Pens up. Ready, go. (Allow 15 secs.) Pens down. Blot the page.

"Attend. Do not look down. In line 5, underline every fraction in which the denominator is not less than the numerator. Pens up. Ready, go. (Allow 15 secs.) Pens down. Blot the page.

"Attend. Do not look down. In line 8, underline all the vowels other than 'o,' 'a,' and 'e.' Pens up. Ready, go. (Allow 15 secs.) Pens down. Blot the page.

"Attend. Do not look down. In line 3, cross out every capital letter that is not immediately preceded by 'e,' 'a' or '7.' Pens up. Ready, go. (Allow 15 secs.) Pens down Blot the page."

TEST 3.

1. a l m x o p e k q r s t f g

2. ! ? : . ; , , ! ! ? ! . , : ;

3. H U M 7 o p 7 B e x 7 b a L

4. h f 4 e s 5 t u i g l o 5 x

5. $\frac{4}{3}$ $\frac{5}{8}$ $\frac{9}{10}$ $\frac{3}{4}$ $\frac{7}{7}$ $\frac{5}{9}$ $\frac{11}{3}$ $\frac{1}{6}$ $\frac{2}{5}$

6. 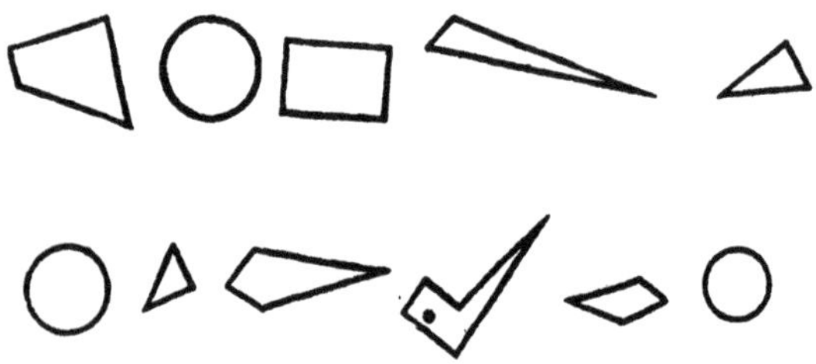

7. 3, 2, 4, 1, 5, 8, 9, 12, 3, 7

8. i e o a i u o e i u a i e a u o o a e i

Do not turn this page until you are told.

TEST 4. 1½ mins.

Learn the following extract with a view to reproducing the ideas contained in it.

Robinson Crusoe made an excellent survey of his island, and felt a legitimate scientific assurance of its thoroughness, a corresponding personal pride also ; but when Friday came, bringing with him a widely different tradition of culture, his fresh survey not only enriched his master's at many a point, but taught him, indeed each of them, its relativity as well. Here indeed is the practical criterion of scientific conclusions, their verifiability by diverse minds. So far then from sneering at Lamarck as an impassioned son of the revolution, at Darwin as a shrewd and prosperous modern Englishman, at Weismann as a German ennobled, and so on, we begin to see how, just as it takes all kinds of people to make a world, so it must also to give anything like a full account of it, to clear these partial accounts up into a science. A science is one of the most collective, most historic, of products ; and most social therefore, though the custodians of its heritage be as yet few.

TEST 4—Continued. 1½ mins.

Learn the following vocabulary :—

type	=	pilu	meat	=	sumib	water	=	borif
coffee	=	savale	wool	=	aksum	cotton	=	monture
shop	=	foleren	cushion	=	entox	rug	=	pirol

TEST 4—Continued. 1½ mins.

Learn the following formulæ :—

$$A = 3UOL + 7LPX - 4YP + 8PEL + 3YFR$$

$$B = 4un + 9ol - 5a - 7RMN^3$$

Do not turn this page until you are told.

TEST 4—Continued. 3 mins.

Write below the extract beginning

Robinson Crusoe

TEST 4—Continued. 1 min.

Write the equivalent for each of the English words :—

cotton ; meat ; type ; shop ; rug ;
water ; wool, ; cushion ; coffee .

TEST 4—Continued. 1 min.

Write the formulæ for A and B :—

A = B =

Close Book A.

October, 1923.

B

Fill in the following and read what is printed below.

	Surname	Christian Names
Name in full:		

	Years	Months
Age:		

The instructions for the tests in this book are printed with each test and also the time allotted. Begin each test when it is announced and stop at the words "Pens down."

Do not Turn this Page until you are Told.

TEST 5. Time 8 mins.

The objects represented on the accompanying sheet (see Fig. 8) may be grouped in a number of ways according to their different characteristics. Make a list of as many different groupings as possible, in which no group contains fewer than four objects. Write down all the positive generalizations which can be made about each of your groups.

[N.B.—The original from which Fig. 8 is reproduced measures 12 in. × 7½ in.]

TEST 6. Time 10 mins.

Two versions (A and B) of eight pieces of prose are given below. Mark with a cross the version which you consider better in each case.

I

A

Unlike ours, English politics,—one hears it on every hand, are pure. Ours unfortunately are known to be not so. The difference seems to be that our politicians will do anything for money and the English politicians won't; they just take the money and won't do a thing for it.

B

Unlike ours, English politics,—one hears it on every hand, —are pure. Unfortunately every one knows that ours are not pure. The difference seems to be that although the English politicians take the money they do nothing for it while our politicians will really do things for money.

II

A

The grey half-tones of daybreak are not the grey half-tones of the day's close, though the degrees of their shade may be the same. In the twilight of the morning light seems active, darkness passive; in the twilight of evening it is the darkness which is active and crescent, and the light which is the drowsy reverse.

B

The greyness of dawn is different from the greyness of evening in quality, although it may be the same in intensity. The difference is that at dawn light seems to be active and darkness seems to be passive while in the evening the reverse is the case.

III

Reflections of a Midget

A

I realized that it is less flattering to compare oneself with the very little things of the world than with the great. For instance, if I were given time I might scale an Alp, but I could show my superiority to an ant only by killing it. Besides, I am beginning to think that one of the pleasantest ways of living is in one's memory. If only I had thought of how beguiling some of my adventures, which I did not enjoy at the time, would appear when recalled, I could have borne them much more easily. Even my old sharpest sorrows are not poignant now and those for whom I sorrowed are asleep.

B

I realized that it is less flattering to compare oneself with the very little things of the world than with the great. Given time, I might scale an Alp ; I could only *kill* an ant. Besides I am beginning to think that one of the pleasantest ways of living is in one's memory. How much less afflicting at times would my present have been if I had had the foresight to remind myself how beguiling it would appear as the past. Even my old sharpest sorrows have now hushed themselves to sleep, and those for whom I have sorrowed are as quiet.

IV

A

You must remember that if you leave your law to judges and your religion to bishops you will soon find yourself without either law or religion. A decent judge or bishop will admit this himself, and his opinion is worth much more than that of a person who does not know what a judge is, or what a bishop is, or what the law is, or what religion is. Your newspaper cannot tell you these things for journalists are too poorly paid in this country to know anything that is fit for publication.

B

Never forget that if you leave your law to judges and your religion to bishops you will presently find yourself without either law or religion. If you doubt this ask any decent judge or bishop. Do *not* ask somebody who does not know what a judge is, or what a bishop is, or what the law is, or what religion is. In other words do not ask your newspaper. Journalists are too poorly paid in this country to know anything that is fit for publication.

V

A

He was an extraordinary old aristocrat who swore like a costermonger, and had the manners of a farmer. I remember seeing him once on Speech-day. He growled at me, gave me a sovereign, and told me not to grow up " a damned Radical " like my father. Cyril had very little affection for him, and was only too glad to spend most of his holidays with us in Scotland. They never really got on together at all. Cyril thought him a bear and he thought Cyril effeminate. He was effeminate, I suppose, in some things, though he was a very good rider and a capital fencer.

B

He was an extraordinary old aristocrat who swore like a costermonger and behaved like a farmer. I remember seeing him one Speech-day when he growled at me, but gave me a sovereign telling me not to grow up " a damned Radical " like my father. Cyril did not care for him much and for this reason was glad to spend most of his holidays with us in Scotland. They did not agree because Cyril thought him a bear and he thought Cyril effeminate. He was effeminate, I suppose, in some things, though he was a very good rider and such a capital fencer that he got the foils before he left Eton.

VI

A

She told him that she read rapidly, "a great deal at one gulp," and thought in flashes as makers of phrases customarily do. She wrote laboriously, however. It was torment to the nervous woman to be unable to cut down, compress and overcharge her thoughts, and she could not do this because she was writing for money.

B

She told him that she read rapidly, " a great deal at one gulp," and thought in flashes—a way with the makers of phrases. She wrote, she confessed, laboriously. The desire to prune, compress, overcharge, was a torment to the nervous woman writing under a sharp necessity for payment.

VII

A

The Prince said, " We have spoken of corruption. I abhor this nugget of bright crystal as much as if it were full of the worms of death. It shocks me as would a gem made from innocent blood. It flashes with hell-fire, as I hold it. I have told you only a small part of its story. One is afraid to imagine for what crime and treacheries it may have been responsible in the past. It has served the powers of hell. I say that there has been enough of disgrace, of broken lives and friendships. All things, good and evil, pestilence and beautiful music, alike come to an end. As for this diamond, God forgive me if I do wrong, I end its empire to-night." The Prince suddenly flung the jewel, which described an arc of light towards the flowing river into which it fell with a flash.

B

" We have spoken of corruption," said the Prince. " To me this nugget is as loathsome as though it were crawling with the worms of death ; it is as shocking as though it were compacted out of innocent blood. I see it here in my hand, and I know it is shining with hell fire. I have told you but a hundrdeth part of its story ; what passed in former ages, to what crimes and treacheries it incited men of yore, the imagination trembles to conceive ; for years and years it has faithfully served the powers of hell ; enough, I say, of blood, enough of disgrace, enough of broken lives and friendships ; all things come to an end, the evil like the good ; pestilence as well as beautiful music ; and as for this diamond, God forgive me if I do wrong, but its empire ends to-night."

The Prince made a sudden movement with his hand, and the jewel, describing an arc of light, dived with a splash into the flowing river.

VIII

A

"Do you not agree with me that it is very difficult to keep thin in this part of the world? Every morning I look in the glass and when I see myself fatter than I was the day before I decide to give up bread and potatoes and to drink hot water. But I dislike hot water very much and as you have doubtless observed, Archdeacon, a man who diets himself is objectionable to all his friends and neighbours. If he refuses the potatoes, his hostess is offended that he does not appreciate what has been grown in her own garden. When he explains that he is dieting, all the other guests make haste to tell stories of what they have done in that line so that the meal is spoiled for every one. I am sure that you have found this the case and I should be interested to hear what you do yourself when you are putting on flesh." The Archdeacon indignantly replied that he did not suffer in that way.

B

"Very difficult to keep thin in this part of the world, isn't ? Every morning when I look at myself in the glass I find myself fatter than I was the day before. Then I say to myself, 'I'll give up bread and potatoes and drink hot water.' Hot water! Loathsome stuff. Moreover, have you noticed, Archdeacon, that a man who diets himself is a perfect nuisance to his friends and neighbours? The moment he refuses potatoes his hostess says to him, 'Why, Mr. Smith, not one of our potatoes! Out of our own garden!' And then he explains to her that he is dieting, whereupon every one at the table hurriedly recites long and dreary histories of how they have dieted at one time or another with this or that success. The meal is ruined for yourself and every one else. Now, isn't it so? What do you do for yourself when you are putting on flesh?"

"I am not aware," said the Archdeacon in his most haughty manner, "that I *am* putting on flesh."

End of Test. *Do not turn this page until you are told.*

TEST 7.—Time 5 mins.

Over each X write the word which makes the best sense. Each X indicates that one, and only one, word has been omitted.

muscle
EXAMPLE. Ralph did not allow a x of his face
heard of this
to indicate that he x one word x x parting address.

The personal power of the king, whatever the theory of absolutism may be, is limited by the hard facts of human nature ; monarchs can rule in person only as much as they can themselves oversee and understand. Hence personal x is for the x part limited to a x circle. A Cæsar or a x may really x the affairs of a x empire, but as a x x the x monarchy has effective existence over a x x area. A conqueror of a x territory has to divest himself of x of his x authority x x . To retain a nominal x he must x it out among his followers or leave the x chiefs in x as tributaries. In either case the ruler of the x province will probably have much x x . Where the native x x things will go on very much x x x x . The distant x will be known as x x x tributes, but in no other x .

End of Test. *Do not turn this page until you are told.*

TEST 8. **Time 8 mins.**

Using the information given below, write all the possible equations, not involving fractions, or the use of negative signs, for the size of the red circle.

The symbols printed under the figures should be employed.

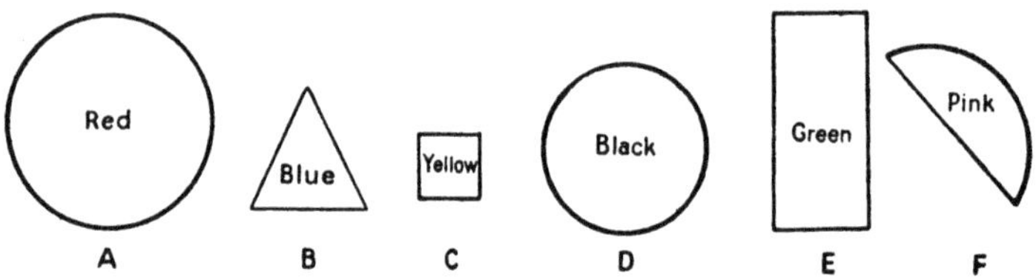

(In the original the figures were coloured.)

The blue triangle is one-fourth of the red circle.

The black circle is five times the yellow square.

The yellow square is one-twelfth of the red circle.

The green rectangle is twice the blue triangle.

The pink segment is one-half the green rectangle.

TEST 9. Time 5 mins.

In each of the following underline the word that is correct as in the examples:

Uncle is to nephew as aunt is to
brother, sister, <u>niece,</u> cousin.

Shell is to nut as skin is to
<u>person,</u> soft, white, coarse.

1. Week is to Thursday as year is to
month, Tuesday, May, season.
2. Pride is to boasting as courage is to
praising, caution, bravado, boldness.
3. Bait is to fish as interest is to
borrower, lender, capital, principal.
4. Talking is to shouting as walking is to
dancing, running, stamping, marching.
5. Twenty-four is to eighteen as thirty-two is to
twenty-seven, twenty-four, eighteen, twenty-eight.
6. Wet is to moisture as foolish is to
silly, folly, fool, stupid.
7. Clock is to hour as thermometer is to
moisture, pressure, temperature, degree.
8. Oak is to willow as stubborn is to
yielding, stolid, weakness, grace.
9. Fire-escape is to building as life-boat is to
passengers, ship, crew, cargo.
10. Silver is to iron as linen is to
wool, cotton, lead, sheets.
11. Fog is to visibility as prejudice is to
fanaticism, truth, conviction, transparence.
12. Conscription is to voluntary service as Prohibition is to
drunkenness, intolerance, temperance, loyalty.
13. This is to that as now is to
soon, here, then, sometime.
14. Possible is to probable as uncertain is to
likely, certain, perhaps, future.
15. Childlike is to childish as boyish is to
pusillanimous, infantile, puerile, innocent.

Administration of the Tests

The tests were given to all the students entering Bedford College, University of London, in the Autumn Term 1921. They were repeated in 1922 and 1923 upon all incoming students, and upon all who had been previously tested. The numbers tested throughout the study are given below.

In 1921, 118 were tested.

In 1922, 204 were tested ; of these 87 had been tested in 1921.

In 1923, 298 were tested ; of these 180 had been tested in 1922, and 87 had been tested in both the previous years.

All the students tested in any one year did exactly the same tests under exactly similar external conditions. The students all did the whole series of tests irrespective of the faculty that they had chosen. The tests were given in the morning of the first Saturday in the Autumn Term ; the whole series occupied a little over an hour. The work of conducting them, giving directions, and timing, was carried out by the staff and students of the Psychology Department. The students who were tested formed a very homogeneous group. They had all passed the London Matriculation or an equivalent examination.[1] With very few exceptions, they were within a year or two of nineteen years of age. They were all women.

[1] Some who had not this standing were tested, but they are not included in the numbers given above, and their results were not used for the statistical work.

CHAPTER III

THE RESULTS

AS the aim of the tests was to distinguish extremes of ability and inability rather than to give the whole group of testees accurately graded positions, the simplest form of marking was adopted. In most tests the solution could be divided into a number of items. The number of items correctly given was taken directly as the mark. The students were graded according to their marks and divided into nine approximately equal classes; the top class was called class 1, the bottom class, 9. All comparisons with college work have been made on the basis of these classes. The data that were obtained seem adequate and quite satisfactory for this part of the work. In a later chapter, however, it will be shown that the form of some of the tests, and various difficulties of accurate marking, lower their reliability and make some of the correlation coefficients of questionable value. In further tests that are to be carried out, it is hoped that these difficulties may be overcome.

Criteria of the usefulness of a given test for practical purposes are not easy to gain in such a case as this. At the outset there are two questions which must be clearly differentiated:

1. Do students who are actually choosing a course in a given faculty score higher or lower in a given test than students who are choosing a course in the other faculty?

2. If students have a low score in a given test, is it unlikely that they will be able to make their way in the faculty to which it is supposed to relate?

The answer to the first question will show if the task set in the test is related to the work of the given faculty. The answer to the second question will determine the importance of the task in the work of the given faculty. In the treatment of the results of individual tests both these questions will be considered.

In the following pages, the terms " top classes " and " bottom classes " will be used. Unless otherwise stated, the former means classes 1 and 2, the latter, classes 8 and 9. As each class comprises approximately 11 per cent. of the testees, the groups that are compared comprise the top and the bottom 22 per cent. respectively. Each of the three successive groups of *incoming* students (but none of those who were being re-tested) was divided into nine classes on the results of each of the tests. It was then possible to put together all the students falling in classes 1 and 2, for example, whatever their year group. It will be noted that this method avoided any confusion that might come through putting together students with different degrees of practice in doing the tests. Apart from some slight irregularities caused by imperfect distributions, the actual number of students in the top classes ranged round 60, and the same for the bottom classes. The worst attenuation occurred in the bottom classes for test 6, which contained only 45 students. The proportion of Arts to Science students in the different classes has been taken as one gauge of the relation of the test to the work of the respective faculties. For instance, if in a test that has been designed for Arts, 80 per cent. of the students in the top classes were Arts students (and only 20 per cent. Science), it would suggest that the test fulfilled its purpose. The suggestion would be strengthened, if in the bottom classes there were only 25 per cent. Arts and 75 per cent. Science. It should be noted that in the following account of performance on the individual tests, no account is taken of the middle 56 per cent. of the students. This is why the percentage of Science or Arts students in the top classes is not necessarily the complement of the percentage of

Science or Arts students in the bottom classes. In the case suggested above, 80 per cent. of the students in the top classes might be Arts, 25 per cent. of the students in the bottom classes, and 45 per cent. of the students in the middle classes ; these proportions would be possible with an equal number of Science and Arts students scattered throughout the whole. In the actual yearly groups there were always more Arts than Science students, but all the figures quoted will be corrected for this disproportion.

There is no simple and satisfactory measure of a student's success in her university work. At the end of the first year all students in London University should pass the Intermediate Examination in either Arts or Science. The marks for this examination have been used in a later section of the present study. They are, however, subject to certain disadvantages as a measure of the students' ability. In the pages that immediately follow, the student will be regarded as belonging, as far as her academic success is concerned, to one of four different classes :

1. Those who fail Intermediate in more than one subject and are therefore obliged to repeat the whole course.
2. Those who fail in one subject—they are "referred," and are obliged to pass in the given subject at a subsequent examination.
3. Those who pass Intermediate and proceed to work for a Pass degree.
4. Those who pass Intermediate and proceed to work for an Honours degree.

These classes do not form a perfect means of grading, but they are the best available. For our purpose the value of the distinction between classes 3 and 4 is the most difficult to gauge. In the past, it was held that only the better students work for an Honours degree and that an Honours degree is more difficult to gain than a Pass. It is very doubtful if either of these assumptions is justified. What may be said, is that no professor would be likely to accept a student who had seemed very dull in her Intermediate Year, for Honours; but with large Intermediate classes it is often impossible for the professor to form a just estimate of an individual's ability. Further, many very able students choose to work for a Pass degree because they do not wish to narrow down their studies and to specialize to the extent that is necessary for Honours. However, it remains true that, on the whole, the brightest students will be found amongst the Honours group and the dullest amongst the Pass.

THE ARTS TESTS.

Speed of Controlled Verbal Association (p. 96, e.g. Write down as many abstract nouns ending in "y" as you can). The test affords the candidate four distinct and unrelated starting points; the task for each series is so simple that none should be affected by lack of any special knowledge. In marking, all words that fulfilled the conditions, received equal credit. It is possible that in some of the tasks, e.g. "words to describe the sea," this militated against the students with a nice sense of the fitness of words, they spent time choosing, where others who were less particular scored through putting down all that came. As far as one can judge, however, the effect of this was unimportant.

Relation to the Work of the Arts Faculty. Sixty per cent. of the students in the top classes (i.e. classes 1 and 2) for the test were Arts students; in the bottom classes (i.e. classes 8 and 9), only thirty-four per cent. were Arts. In other words, nearly twice as many Arts students do well on the test as do badly, and the reverse is true of the Science students. These figures suggest that the ability measured by the test is to some extent related to the work of the Arts faculty. The important question. remains: "Do Arts students who score well in this test do better in their College work than Arts students who score badly?" The following table answers this question.

Arts Students.	In test classes 1 and 2.	In test classes 8 and 9.
No. accepted for Honours degrees	28	5
,, ,, ,, Pass ,,	2	7
,, failed Intermediate in one subject	1	3
,, ,, ,, in more than one subject	4	6

It shows that 85 per cent. of the Arts students in the top classes are accepted for either Honours or Pass work in the Arts faculty, while only 57 per cent. of those in the bottom classes are accepted. Further, whereas in the top classes 28 of the future Honours students are to be found, only 5 are to be found in the bottom classes.

Judging from these results the test has value for the purpose for which it was designed. It is hoped that in future work it may be improved in the light of the experience that has been gained from the present study.

Ability to Recall (pp. 99). It was suggested that memory is of more importance in the work of the Arts student than in that of the Science student. Test 4 was, therefore, designed to measure the candidate's memory for different kinds of material; prose passage, nonsense vocabulary, and nonsense formulæ. The prose passage was marked both for number of words correctly reproduced and also for number of ideas. As the correlation between the two was very high it is unnecessary to treat them separately. In the nonsense vocabulary and formulæ each item correctly reproduced gained a mark. In the results for the test as a whole, Arts and Science students are in equal proportions in classes 1 and 2. In classes 8 and 9 there are 60 per cent. Science to 40 per cent. Arts. The difference in the proportions is not sufficient to suggest that ability to recall is more essentially related to the work of the one faculty than to that of the other. Arts students did very slightly better in the memory for vocabulary than did the Science, and the Science did very slightly better than the Arts in the memory for formulæ.

A study of the top and bottom classes for this test affords further evidence for the claim that was made in Part I as to the relation between memory and intelligence. Of those who are in the top classes for memory, 29 per cent. are also in the top classes for general capacity and only 10 per cent. in the bottom classes. Of those in the bottom classes for memory, 50 per cent. are also in the bottom classes for general capacity and only 10 per cent. in the top classes. In other words, an individual with a very poor memory is five times as likely to have an inferior intelligence as is an individual with a good memory. At the same time, a good memory is not as frequently accompanied by high intelligence as is a poor memory by low intelligence. These statistics are confirmed in the results of an independent study that was carried out upon a group of 108 girls of school-leaving age. They are a confirmation of what was suggested in Part I with regard to confluence as the measure of intelligence. The person with a good memory may, or may not, have the degree of confluence essential for high general intelligence. The person with a poor memory, almost certainly lacks it. Some, thinking of the notorious forgetfulness and absent-mindedness of geniuses, will challenge this statement. But reflection will show that such absent-mindedness is no proof of a poor memory, only of lack of interest in the things that others think should interest the genius. It is not safe to conclude that anyone has a poor memory until he has been accurately tested over a wide range of material.

In the later sections the test will not be treated as an Arts test.

Judgment of Style (pp. 102–6).—In Test 6 the candidate was asked to discriminate between each of eight pairs of prose passages from the point of view of style. Each pair consisted of a quotation from a standard author and a mauled version of this quotation. The mauling consisted in weakening the force of the passage and spoiling its æsthetic value. The sense and correct grammatical constructions were retained in the mauled versions. It was not possible to establish the validity of the experimenter's judgment by using the test with a very large number of people in a preliminary trial, but the independent judgment of several specialists in English was obtained. It seems probable that the mauled versions erred on the side of being too crude, as the experimenter was anxious to avoid questions of individual taste and such nice questions of style as would involve special training. From the point of view of scoring, the test was weak as it gave only nine possibilities (0–8), and as each mark signified the candidate's choice between two things, by chance alone he would often gain between four and six of these nine points. As, however, the test was designed merely to pick out those very lacking in appreciation of style, this was not thought to be a serious drawback, and considerations of time and simplicity of marking made a more elaborate test or method of marking undesirable at this stage. The candidates in classes 8 and 9 had only from 0–3 correct judgments out of eight, those in classes 1 and 2, had 7 or 8.

Relation to the Work of the Arts Faculty. In the top classes there were 50 per cent. Arts, and 50 per cent. Science students. In the bottom classes there were 48 per cent. Arts and 52 per cent. Science students. The following table shows that the Arts students who do well in the test do better in their College work than the Arts students who do badly.

Arts Students.	In test classes 1 and 2.	In test classes 8 and 9.[1]
No. accepted for Honours degrees	25 . . .	10
,, ,, ,, Pass ,, ...	2 . . .	4
,, failed Intermediate in one subject : . . .	1 . . .	5
,, ,, ,, in more than one subject	4 . . .	3

Thus 84 per cent. of those in the top classes and only 64 per cent. of those in the bottom classes proceed to higher degrees. From the two top classes more than twice as many proceed to Honours as from the bottom classes; this is true even when allowance has been made for the attenuation of the bottom class, see p. 112.

[1] The numbers given are those actually obtained. In the diagram, p. 122, they are corrected for the attenuation of the class.

A modification of this test has been devised which will permit of finer and more accurate grading. It is hoped that this may serve to throw light on the importance of this special ability in the work of the faculty of arts.

The Science Tests

Drawing to Directions and Solution of Maze Problems (pp. 92–95).—Experimental work in the sciences involves the grasping of spatial relations and ready orientation. The simple problems of this test were designed to measure the candidate's capacity in this direction. The drawings and the mazes were marked according to the number of correct turns taken, marks being deducted for errors committed, whether they were corrected or not. No account was taken of neatness.

Relation to the Work of the Faculty.—In the top classes for this test 75 per cent. of the students were from the Science faculty, in the bottom classes 27 per cent. The following table shows the relative success of Science students in the top and the bottom classes respectively.

Science Students.	In test classes 1 and 2.	In test classes 8 and 9.
No. accepted for Honours degrees	25	6
,, ,, ,, Pass ,,	10	4
,, failed Intermediate in one subject	2	1
,, ,, ,, in more than one subject	4	4

Thus 85 per cent of the Science students in the top classes, and 63 per cent. of those in the bottom classes succeed in their college work. From the top classes approximately four times as many proceed to Honours in science as from the bottom classes.

Ability to carry out Directions given Orally (pp. 97–8).—No doubt the specialist in science will smile at the suggestion that the ability to carry out directions from memory is an element in scientific ability. Reflection, however, will probably convince him that this ability is likely to be one of the humbler tools making for success in his work. In the laboratory work of the comparatively elementary student it is certainly an important factor.

Relation to the Work of the Faculty.—In the top classes for this test 73 per cent., and in the bottom classes 28 per cent. were Science students. The following table shows the relative success of Science students in the top and bottom classes respectively.

Science Students.	In test classes 1 and 2.	In test classes 8 and 9.
No. accepted for Honours degrees	33	9
„ „ „ Pass „	8	4
„ failed Intermediate in one subject	1	1
„ „ „ in more than one subject	0	4

It will be seen that practically all the Science students in classes 1 and 2 succeed in the work of the Science faculty; 72 per cent. of those in classes 8 and 9 succeed. Four times as many of the future Science Honours students come from the top classes as from the bottom.

Ability to Classify and to Generalize (p. 101).—In all the sciences, but more particularly in the biological, the student is likely to be faced with a mass of concrete material which must be classified and understood in relation to general principles. Test 5 was invented to serve as a criterion of the student's ability to do this. Reference to the coloured sheet facing p. 101 will show that the material to be classified consisted of a variety of coloured shapes with diverse markings and appendages. Obviously they could be classified in a number of different ways, according, for example, to colour, form, size, markings, etc. The experimenter was astonished at the large number who failed to hit upon any comprehensive plan of classification. It was rather the exception than the rule, to find such headings as have been suggested above systematically applied. When the test was planned it was thought that the test of initiative that it involves (in devising classifications) would be a valuable criterion

9

of the student's ability. It probably is, but like all tests that permit of individual choice of procedure, the test in its present form is very difficult to mark. In future it will be modified in order to overcome this difficulty.

Relation to the Work of the Science Faculty.—In the top classes 60 per cent. are Science students, in the bottom classes, 24 per cent. No Science student in the bottom two classes ranks above class 5 on the general capacity tests, i.e. they are all below average in general capacity. This and the fact that only 60 per cent. of the top class are Science students suggests that the test measures general capacity to a fairly high degree. It will be seen from the Correlations on p. 138 that it also involves the kind of facility with language that is measured by Test 2.

Table showing the relative success of the Science students in the top and the bottom classes respectively.

Science Students.	In test classes 1 and 2.	In test classes 8 and 9.
No. accepted for Honours degrees	23	5
„ „ „ Pass „	11	2
„ failed Intermediate in one subject	1	1
„ „ „ in more than one subject	0	5

Of the Science students in the top classes 97 per cent. are successful in their college work; only 54 per cent. of those in the bottom classes are successful. Over four times as many students proceed to Honours from the top classes as from the bottom classes. It is to be noted that while there are signs that the test measures general capacity rather more than the other science tests that have been described, the fact that the proportion of Science to Arts students in the bottom classes is as one to four suggests that the ability involved is related to the work of the Science faculty.

Ability to Use Symbols in Relation to Space and Number (p. 108).—Problems similar to that involved in this test are constantly arising in Physics and Mathematics, and even in Chemistry there are problems that are somewhat similar. At first sight it may seem to the non-mathematical person to involve difficult calculations, but in reality the mathematical relations are extremely simple and should present no difficulty whatever to a student who has passed a university entrance examination. The real problem lies in substituting the given symbols for the verbal descriptions, and in using the symbols consistently. The problem is so simple that one would expect, out of such a selected group, to find none who would not frame at least five or six of the easier equations. Actually, the highest number of equations given by anyone in class 9 (taking into account all the groups throughout the three years) was 4, and the average number of correct equations given by candidates in class 9 was 1·5. In class 1, the highest number ever given was 27, and the average was 18·9.

Relation to the Work of the Science Faculty.—Seventy-two per cent. of the students in the top classes, and 25 per cent. of those in the bottom classes are Science students.

Table showing the relative success of the Science students in the top and bottom classes respectively.

Science Students.	In test classes 1 and 2.	In test classes. 1 and 9.
No. accepted for Honours degrees	33	6
,, ,, ,, Pass ,,	9	6
,, failed Intermediate in one subject	0	1
,, ,, ,, in more than one subject	5	4

Eighty-one per cent. of the Science students in the top classes succeed in their work in the science faculty, 70 per cent. of those in the bottom classes succeed. From the top classes 33 Science students proceed to Honours, from the bottom classes 6 proceed to Honours.

ERRATUM

The explanation at the foot of Fig. 9 should read:

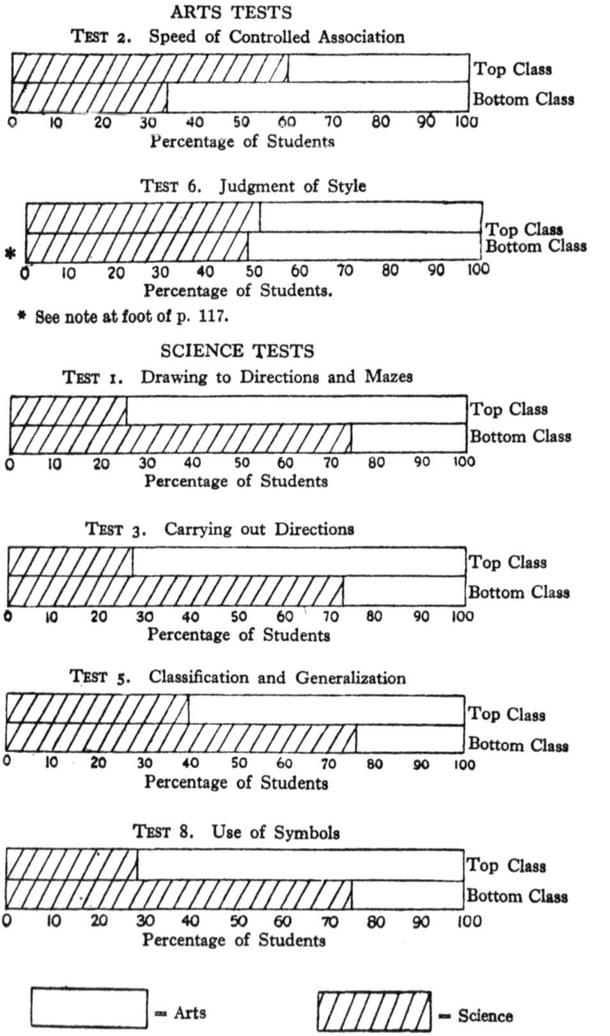

FIG. 9.—Diagram showing the Relative Position of Arts and Science Students in the Test Results.

CONCLUSIONS WITH REGARD TO THE SCIENCE AND ARTS TESTS

From the evidence that has been given it seems fair to conclude that each of the science tests measure a special ability that is involved more in the work of the science, than in that of the arts faculty. In the results for each test there are approximately three times as many Arts as Science students in the bottom classes; there are between four and five times as many of the future Science Honours students in the top as in the bottom classes.[1] At the same time it is true that amongst the group who do very badly in each of the tests, there are a few who proceed to Honours in Science. This is, of course, to be expected. A lack in any one of these narrow special abilities may be counterbalanced by a high degree of general capacity or of other special abilities. This is not meant to imply the view that was opposed in an earlier section (see p. 45). It does not mean that the same activity is accomplished by certain factors in ability in one case, and by other factors in another, but only that a student who does one part or aspect of his work badly, may do so well in other parts or aspects that the weakness is unimportant for the whole. One of the candidates was an outstanding illustration of this. On the tests she did exceptionally well in all but drawing to directions and mazes. Having marked the tests and been struck with the superiority of this student, the experimenter began asking questions about her work in the science faculty, before the end of the first term. The replies were not at all enthusiastic. All the departments in which she worked complained of her incompetence in practical work, and had failed to note any exceptional ability. As time went on, their opinion changed and they agreed that in spite

[1] It is, of course, recognized that differences in general capacity help to account for this, but see below, p. 129.

of her marked lack of ability in handling apparatus, she accomplished very good work. At the end of her first year, every one of the lecturers under whom she had worked would have been glad to accept her for Honours in his subject. While the lack of one or even two special abilities *may* be compensated in this way, it seems unlikely that a student lacking in more than one of them will succeed in the work of the science faculty.

Of the three tests which it was thought might serve in relation to arts, test 4 (memory) may be definitely eliminated. The test of speed of verbal association does not discriminate for arts as well as the best science tests discriminate for science, but even in its present form, the results show that an Arts student is twice as likely to be in the top classes as in the bottom, and that seven times as many students from the top as from the bottom classes proceed to Honours in Arts. The test of judgment of style is too general in character, and inadequate from the point of view of marking. It is hoped that these drawbacks may be overcome in a new form of the test that is being planned.

A priori, it seems probable that, particularly for women, special abilities will not affect the work of the arts faculty as much as work in science. For if we take the view that special abilities are all determined by degree of general capacity plus familiarity with the specific material, it is obvious that the activities of the Arts students are much more uniform as regards their degree of familiarity for different individuals, than are the activities of the science faculty and that therefore, general capacity will be the chief factor determining the differences between individuals. It has been shown that, on the average, girls do not gain in their earlier years as good a mastery over spatial relations as do boys. At the same time they vary very much amongst themselves in regard to this ability. Thus, in their case at any rate, it is likely to figure as an important special ability. The other abilities important for science also involve activities which have not been repeated to the point of absolute familiarity, as certainly as have the activities involved in the work of the arts faculty. In the arts faculty it is compulsory for the student to study at least two languages. As girls' schools tend, to a greater degree than boys' schools, to specialize in language, this again makes it likely that the girls' work in the arts faculty will be more a measure of their general capacity than of differing degrees of familiarity with the material. It may be that had these tests been carried out in a college for men, the arts tests would have proved more, the science tests less, satisfactory. It is to be noted that the activity that does appear to be definitely related to work in arts (rapidity of verbal association) is an instance of an activity that is very dependent upon experience during the main developmental period, see p. 57 f.

Tests of General Capacity

The two tests that were used as "general" were the Prose Completion (see p. 107) and Analogies (see p. 109). Unfortunately there are no standardized variants of these suitable for university students, and it was not possible to try the tests devised for the present study with a large group in order to test their suitability, although the opinion of several independent judges was gained. The results show that the Prose Completion tended, in each case, to be too difficult, and as it consisted of one continuous passage, this meant that the less intelligent students who lost the clue near the beginning had not an adequate chance of showing what they could do. The Analogies test was a little too easy. In each case the mean was approximately 9 out of a possible 15 marks, with a standard deviation of 3. While these defects make it difficult to use the results for more elaborate statistical operations, they do not invalidate the distinction that may be drawn between students in the top and the bottom classes, respectively, as in both tests the students in the top classes do from four to five times as well as the students in the bottom classes.

In the Prose Completion the Arts students did distinctly better than the Science; in the Analogies, the results showed practically no difference between Science and Arts. This would lead one to conjecture that linguistic ability is involved to a much greater degree in the former than in the latter. One would, of course, have guessed this, but it is not usually recognized when Prose Completion is used as a test of "general ability." Rapidity of verbal association is likely to help in prose completion, and as the former ability is more specific to arts than science it is natural that prose completion should be also.

The Results of Combining the Individual Tests to Form Arts, Science, and General Groups Respectively

When the arts tests are combined there are 65 per cent. Arts to 35 per cent. Science students in the top classes, and 36 per cent. Arts to 64 per cent. Science in the bottom classes. These proportions are practically the same as those found for the speed of verbal association test. This is not surprising in view of the fact that the other arts test (judgment of style), does not, in its present form, serve to discriminate between science and arts. Thus combining these two arts tests does not give a finer measure of discrimination than is given by the test for speed of verbal association alone.

When the science tests are combined there are 74 per cent. Science students to 26 per cent. Arts in the top classes, and 17 per cent. Science to 83 per cent. Arts in the bottom classes. Thus the combination of the science tests leads to a more perfect means of discrimination between science and arts ability than is afforded by any individual science test.

A COMPARISON OF INTER-B.A. AND INTER-B.SC. RESULTS. WITH THE RESULTS OF TESTS IN ARTS, SCIENCE, AND "GENERAL ABILITY"

At the end of the first year in the University, students take the Intermediate Examination in their respective faculties. On the whole, their performance on this affords the most finely graded criterion of academic success that can be obtained. In later work the specialization and smallness of the numbers studying any one subject make comparison very difficult. At the same time, it must be admitted that in marking the papers for the Intermediate Examination examiners do not aim at drawing very fine distinctions—it is only a pass or fail examination. Further, the numerical value of the pass mark is not the same for all subjects, so that the marks for different subjects cannot be compared until certain adjustments have been made. After a consideration of all these difficulties it was decided to express the amount to which the student's performance came above or below the pass mark as a plus or minus fraction of the pass mark. For instance, if the pass mark in a given subject was 40 and a student gained 50 marks, he would have gained 10 above pass, and this is ·25 of the pass mark. If he had had 30 marks, that would have been expressed as —·25. The three subjects most commonly taken in arts and science respectively were used for this purpose. The average Intermediate marks for the students in the top and bottom classes in the arts, science, and general tests were calculated. The following table shows the results.

The Performance in the Arts Intermediate Examination of:

A. Arts Students in Classes, 1, 2, and 3 on the Arts Tests.

Year.	Latin.	English.	French
1922	·3	·2	·2
1923	·4	·4	·2
1924	·2	·2	·2
Average	·3	·26	·2

B. Arts Students in Classes, 7, 8, and 9 on the Arts Tests.

1922	·2	·1	·1
1923	·2	·1	·1
1924	·1	·1	·1
Average	·16	·1	·1

C. Arts Students in Classes, 1, 2, and 3 on the General Tests.

1922	·3	·2	·2
1923	·3	·2	·1
1924	·3	·3	·3
Average	·3	·23	·2

D. Arts Students in Classes, 7, 8, and 9 on the General Tests.

1922	·2	·1	·1
1923	·3	·2	·1
1924	·1	·1	·1
Average	·2	·13	·1

The Performance in the Science Intermediate Examination of :

A. Science Students in Classes 1, 2, and 3, on the Science Tests.

Year.	Chemistry.	Physics.	Mathematics.
1922	·7	·5	·5
1923	·7	·5	·6
1924	·7	·7	·7
Average	·7	·56	·6

B. Science Students in Classes 7, 8, and 9 on the Science Tests.

Year.	Chemistry.	Physics.	Mathematics.
1922	·4	·6	·3
1923	·6	·5	·2
1924	·0	·0	—·2
Average	·33	·36	·1

C. Science Students in Classes 1, 2, and 3 on the General Tests.

1922	·4	·4	·4
1923	·9	·7	·5
1924	·6	·7	·8
Average	·63	·6	·56

D. Science Students in Classes 7, 8, and 9, on the General Tests.

1922	·5	·6	·5
1923	·6	·5	·4
1924	·4	·5	·4
Average	·5	·53	·43

A study of these tables brings out the following facts.

A. With Regard to Arts Students :

1. Arts students in the top classes of the arts tests gain 2·1 times as many marks above the pass mark in the Arts Intermediate, as the Arts students in the bottom classes.

2. Arts students in the top classes of the general tests gain 1·7 as many marks above the pass mark in the Arts Intermediate, as the Arts students in the bottom classes.

3. Therefore the arts tests are roughly 25 per cent. better than the general tests as a gauge of the students' success in the work of the arts faculty.

B. With Regard to Science Students :

1. Science students in the top classes for the science tests gain 2·3 times as many marks above the pass mark in the Science Intermediate as the Science students in the bottom classes.

2. Science students in the top classes for the general tests gain 1·2 times as many marks above the pass mark in Science Intermediate as Science students in the bottom classes.

3. Therefore the science tests are roughly 100 per cent. better than the general tests as a gauge of the students' success in the work of the science faculty.

These results do not throw any direct light upon the relation of success in science and arts tests to success in general tests. The following table gives data for the consideration of this problem. In the Table the results for all students, whether working in the Arts or in the Science Faculty are taken together.

Students in Top Classes (1 and 2) for General Tests.

Percentage who were in top classes for both Arts and Science	13
,, ,, bottom ,, ,, ,, ,,	0
,, ,, top ,, ,, Science	40
,, ,, bottom ,, ,, ,,	9
,, ,, top ,, ,, Arts	40
,, ,, bottom ,, ,, ,,	4
,, ,, top ,, ,, either A. or Sc.	79
,, ,, bottom ,, ,, ,, ,,	13

Students in Bottom Classes (8 and 9) for General Tests.

Percentage who were in top classes for both Arts and Science	2
,, ,, bottom ,, ,, ,, ,,	22
,, ,, top ,, ,, Science	8
,, ,, bottom ,, ,, ,,	37
,, ,, top ,, ,, Arts	10
,, ,, bottom ,, ,, ,,	47
,, ,, top ,, ,, either A. or Sc.	17
,, ,, bottom ,, ,, ,, ,,	60

This table shows that the student who has good results for the test of general ability is about five times as likely to have outstanding special ability as is the student who has poor results. In terms of the theory developed in Part 1 this means that the individual in whom there is a high degree of confluence as judged by his work in material that is very generally familiar is five times as likely to have developed a special aptitude for the work involved in either the science or the arts tests, as is a student for whom the measure of confluence is low. The table also shows that while only 13 per cent. of those who are in the top classes for general ability stand well in both science and arts tests, 79 per cent. excel in one or the other. This is evidence for the importance of testing for special abilities. The picture of those who stand in the bottom classes on the general tests is dismal. Only

17 per cent. stand in the top classes for either science or arts tests, and only 2 per cent. stand in the top classes for both. It must be remembered, however, that this table gives only the extremes and that although few of those who are low in general ability excel in arts or science, many (40 per cent.) are above the average (class 5) in either arts or science tests. Here again is evidence for the need of testing special abilities.

CHAPTER IV

THE EFFECT OF PRACTICE AND COACHING

THE results that have been presented justify the conclusion that the science tests are tests of abilities that are involved in the work of the science courses, and that speed of controlled verbal association is related to success in the arts courses. Allowing that there are these special abilities, the next question that arises is whether or no they are easily acquired. If they are easily acquired, then a student who lacks them need not necessarily be deterred from taking the relevant course; if they are not easily acquired, the student who lacks them is liable to have difficulty. One way of attacking the problem is to compare the grades made by Science students in science tests for two or more successive years, and the same for Arts students in arts tests. If the abilities can be acquired in a short time one would expect the students to improve in the tests related to the faculty in which they are working. For purposes of comparison, a group of 141 students will be taken. They all took the 1922 and the 1923 tests, and with regard to their work in their respective faculties they form a very homogeneous group. Of these students 56 were Science and 85 were Arts; 73 of them had also taken the tests in 1921, and for these the results of the 1921 test were compared with the results of the 1923. Thus more than half the group had had two years of work in either arts or science, between the two series of tests. The Arts students average class 4 for the speed of controlled verbal association, in judgment of style, they average class 5, on both the first and the last occasions. Thus, in neither of these tests did practice have an effect. The Science students average class 4–5 in each of the science tests and in each year. The following table, however, shows that there is a slight improvement on each test, not amounting to the difference of a whole class.

Average Class attained by Science Students on Science Tests on first and last occasions of Testing.

	Class on first occasion.	Class on last occasion.
Drawings and Mazes	4·5	4·3
Oral Directions	4·5	4·4
Classification &c	5·0	4·5
Use of symbols	4·5	4·2

The greatest difference occurs in the classification test. It amounts to ·5 of a class which (there being nine classes) is 5½ per cent.

Having ascertained that the work in the science faculty and practice in working the science tests themselves had a very small though consistent effect on the students' performance, the experimenter was interested to ascertain whether or no specific coaching would have an effect. For this purpose it seemed desirable to work with a group to whom the tests would be quite new. The Principal of St. Katherine's Training College, Tottenham, was approached, and she very kindly gave permission for the experiment to be carried out on a class of first year students.[1] Miss Margaret McFarlane, B.A., Ph.D., planned the method of coaching and conducted the experiment. The whole group was given the tests in the same form and manner as they had been given to the Bedford College students in 1922. The group was then coached in two

[1] I wish to take this opportunity of thanking the staff and students of St. Katherine's for the kind co-operation which made the experiment possible.

sections;[1] one section in Tests 1–4, the other in Tests 5–9. At the end, all the students were given the whole series as it had been given in 1923 to the Bedford College students. The coaching consisted in:

1. A preliminary talk explaining the purpose and plan of the given test; and essentials of attitude (e.g. maximum of attention during practice).

2. Practice, including short discussions of the best methods of setting about each test, and actual practice on similar material.

Sixty-three students completed the experiment, thirty of these were in one section (A), thirty-three in the other (B). For all the tests, in both the preliminary and the final series, the sixty-three students were ranked. The average rank of each section in the preliminary trial was then compared with the average rank of each section in the final trial. This method was adopted because it avoids any difficulty that might arise from inequality of difficulty in the test material, or in the average general capacity of the groups. If the coaching has been effective the section (A) that has been coached in Tests 1–4, should have higher average ranks in these tests in the final trial than in the preliminary, and the other section (B) will then necessarily have lower ranks on the final than the preliminary, for what one section gains the other must lose in ranks. Similarly, the effect of coaching on Tests 5–9 may be gauged by the comparison of the preliminary and the final average ranks of section B. From the following table it may be seen that, as a matter of fact, there was very little difference between the two groups on the preliminary trial, for as there were 63 ranks in all, any normal group selected from the rest should have an average rank of about 31·5. It will be seen that in the preliminary trial both sections approximated to this on all tests except Classification.

[1] Time table arrangements made it impossible to divide the group so as to have two sections of approximately equal general capacity, but it will be seen that the results were treated in such a way as to avoid any error arising from inequality in general capacity, in as far as such existed.

Average Ranks of A Division for Tests on which it was Coached.

	Prel. Trial	Final Trial
1. Mazes and Drawings	30	25
2. Speed of verbal association	32·5	26·9
3. Directions	33·6	31·6
4. Memory	32·6	32·1

Thus coaching led to an improvement of 17 per cent. on Test 1, 16 per cent. on Test 2, 6 per cent. on Test 3, and no appreciable improvement on Test 4.

Average Ranks of B Division for Tests on which it was Coached.

	Prel. Trial.	Final Trial.
5. Classification	27·5	31·5
6. Judgment of Style	32·7	25·5
7. Use of Symbols	33·2	26·7
8. Prose Completion	33·4	29
9. Analogies	32·1	30·3

With this Division coaching led to an apparent loss on Test 5, a gain of 22 per cent. on Test 6, 19 per cent. on Test 7, 13 per cent. on Test 8, 5½ per cent. on Test 9. The paradoxical result for Test 5 is due to the fact that owing presumably to chance circumstances, the A Division did very poorly in the preliminary trial, whereas in the final trial their performance was average. A study of the actual work done by the B Division throughout the experiment, suggests that there was improvement. In particular, four or five students who had been quite floored by the test on the first occasion did quite creditably on the last.

While the comparatively small numbers involved, and the limited time for coaching, make it absurd to attach great importance to the figures that have been quoted, they are sufficiently consistent with themselves, and harmonious with known facts, to be of interest. If we omit the Classification Test, the other results suggest that the improvement is roughly in inverse proportion to the novelty of the activity involved. The exception to this is the small improvement of $5\frac{1}{2}$ per cent. on Analogies. This is not due, as might be supposed, to the test being too easy (see p. 125), for the distribution for each trial shows that the test was not too easy for this group. The explanation must be that, while the exact form of the Analogies Test is certainly novel, all the material is so familiar and fundamental to all activity, that the preliminary trial gauges with very fair accuracy the testees' maximum ability. In other words, we are confirmed, from another point of view, in regarding Analogies as a good test of General Capacity, and as better than Prose Completion for this purpose.

It will be noted that, on the whole, the improvement with coaching is greater than one might have expected from the very slight improvement with practice noted in the case of the Bedford College students. With regard to this, two facts should be borne in mind. In the first place, the coaching is much more specific to the tests than is the work of the students studying for degrees. In the second place, as the latter have all passed matriculation or its equivalent, the work involved in the tests is not as novel to them on the first occasion as it is likely to be for at least a number of the St. Katherine's group. The very fact that the degree students have been through a more rigorous process of selection before entering college makes it improbable that mere novelty in the tests will affect their results to as great a degree as it will those of a group that has, on the whole, been selected by a less difficult examination. Taking all the facts into account, it does not seem likely that students who are seriously lacking in the special abilities involved in the science tests will acquire them with sufficient ease for the choice of a science course to be advisable for them. The same seems to be true of the one arts test, for which at present we have adequate evidence, viz. speed of verbal association.

CHAPTER V

CORRELATIONS

IT has been stated in an earlier section that in this preliminary study of special abilities the experimenter aimed throughout at drawing the broad distinction of "good" or "bad" with regard to the testees' performance on each test rather than at grading the group accurately. It has been shown that, on the whole, this aim was achieved. We are now to consider the value of the data from the point of view of the finer grading which is influential in determining the coefficients of correlation. Let us consider first the reliability coefficients which show how the results for one application of a given test correlate with another application of the same test. In the following Table the highest and the lowest for any group on each test is given together with the Probable Error.

Reliability Coefficients

Test.	Highest.	Lowest.
1.	·563 ±·084	·428 ±·057
2.	·652 ±·071	·53 ±·05
3.	·599 ±·044	·588 ±·080
4.	·759 ±·049	·501 ±·052
5.	·289 ±·064	·176 ±·119
6.	·511 ±·091	·294 ±·064
7.	·473 ±·095	·137 ±·068
8.	·625 ±·071	·366 ±·060
9.	·562 ±·080	·306 ±·063

These are correlations computed by the Pearson

CORRELATIONS. (Pearson Formula), 1st Year, 1923

No. of Test.	1A	1B	2	3	4	5	6	7	8	9
1A	—	·097 ± ·061	—·014 ± ·062	·234 ± ·059	—·242 ± ·058	·004 ± ·062	·053 ± ·062	—·020 ± ·062	·181 ± ·060	—·013 ± ·062
1B	·097 ± ·061	—	·046 ± ·062	·114 ± ·061	—·054 ± ·062	·189 ± ·060	·033 ± ·062	·073 ± ·062	·286 ± ·057	·122 ± ·061
2	—·014 ± ·062	·046 ± ·062	—	—·058 ± ·062	·147 ± ·061	·244 ± ·058	·111 ± ·061	·177 ± ·060	—·034 ± ·062	·121 ± ·061
3	·234 ± ·059	·114 ± ·061	—·058 ± ·062	—	·104 ± ·061	·202 ± ·060	—·017 ± ·062	·109 ± ·061	·088 ± ·062	·014 ± ·062
4	—·242 ± ·058	—·054 ± ·062	·147 ± ·061	·104 ± ·061	—	·175 ± ·060	—·054 ± ·062	·213 ± ·059	·010 ± ·062	·200 ± ·060
5	·004 ± ·062	·189 ± ·060	·244 ± ·058	·202 ± ·060	·175 ± ·060	—	—·046 ± ·062	·225 ± ·059	·181 ± ·060	·199 ± ·060
6	·053 ± ·062	·033 ± ·062	·111 ± ·061	—·017 ± ·062	—·054 ± ·062	—·046 ± ·062	—	—·129 ± ·061	·004 ± ·062	·073 ± ·062
7	·020 ± ·062	·073 ± ·062	·177 ± ·060	·109 ± ·061	·213 ± ·059	·225 ± ·059	—·129 ± ·061	—	·055 ± ·062	·179 ± ·060
8	·181 ± ·060	·286 ± ·057	—·034 ± ·062	·088 ± ·062	·010 ± ·062	·181 ± ·060	·004 ± ·062	·055 ± ·062	—	·245 ± ·058
9	—·013 ± ·062	·122 ± ·061	·121 ± ·061	·014 ± ·062	·200 ± ·060	·199 ± ·060	·073 ± ·062	·179 ± ·060	·245 ± ·058	—

formula. The smallness of the coefficients for Tests 5, 6 and 7 rests on grounds that have been indicated in the account of the results for the individual tests. It is hoped that by the improvements that have been planned, the reliability coefficients for these tests may be raised considerably. The coefficients as a whole are not as high as are sometimes found. To account for this the following facts should be considered :

1. The time given to each individual test was necessarily short. This means that chance circumstances tell upon the results much more than they would over a longer period. (For example, a hair on one's pen nib has a more serious effect on a two-minute than on a five-minute test.)

2. The tests were a year apart, which gives time for considerable changes in conditions of health, etc.

3. With groups as highly selected as these were, very high correlations are unlikely because a very slight difference in the absolute performance of a student may make an important difference in relative position in the group.

4. The tests given on the different occasions had not been standardized. While every care was taken to make them as similar as possible it is almost inevitable that some of the variations would introduce difficulties affecting some individuals more than others.

Taking all these facts into account it seems likely that with standardization and the improvements that have been planned with regard to individual tests, it may be possible to raise their reliability considerably.

Inter-Correlations

The inter-correlations of tests are given on p. 138. They are all very low and the majority are negligible. Thus they suggest that the abilities measured by the tests are special and unrelated. It is probably unjustifiable to found any conclusions of a theoretical nature upon such small coefficients. The coefficients of Partial Correlation have, however, been computed from them; any difference between the original coefficient and the coefficient of partial correlation that was found was very slight. This would be interpreted to mean that the correlations in the Table are due to the nature of the individual tests of each pair and are not brought about to any important degree by the influence of a factor shared by them with other tests, such as general capacity. The fact that the group of students is already highly selected would make this result probable a priori.

In an attempt to analyse the results still further the following procedure was adopted. The students for all three years were divided into two groups according to the Faculty, Arts or Science, in which they were working. The inter-correlations for each of these groups were worked separately, using the students' Standard Deviations instead of actual marks, in order to avoid inequalities due to differences in the years. The differences between the correlations for the two groups were quite negligible. For the Science group the correlations of test 6 (Judgment of Style) became negative with all the other tests with the exception of tests 5 (Classification) and 9 (Analogies), whereas those for the Arts group were positive for all except test 5. This was the only result of any interest, but here again the coefficients are so small that nothing can be based upon them until the tests have been tried again. It is a point to which attention will be directed in future work.

CHAPTER VI

CONCLUSION

IN the work that has been described it is obvious that only the fringe of the problem of the special abilities involved in Science and Arts has been touched. The study did not aim at a complete analysis, but at finding those abilities that are most important from the point of view of success in academic work. No doubt there are many abilities other than those found that are important in this way. Further it is not claimed that those that have been found are simple and unitary. In accordance with the argument of Part I the writer inclines to the view that each test measures a compound of several influences : the basal general capacity of the testee plus his familiarity with a number of different forms of experience. In such a simple task as the Directions Test involves, the answers to each of the following questions, and many others, will have its effect upon the testee's result :

1. Is he practised and disciplined in listening ?
2. Has he a good memory for things heard ? Strong after-images might even help here.
3. Is he familiar with the symbols and forms in relation to which the directions are to be carried out ?

Indeed on the theory that has been developed we should expect every change and variety of material to correspond with a so-called special ability, so that any attempt to arrive at a list of ultimate and clearly distinguishable special abilities would seem futile.

The fact that it has been easier to find tests for Science

than for Arts calls for some remark. It seems to have arisen from two causes. In the first place the fact that every science subject involves practical work means that these subjects have a certain number of requirements in common, and even in their theoretical aspects there is a very considerable degree of interdependence and overlapping, although it *may* not be more than with Arts subjects. In the second place special abilities that are almost certainly involved in Arts subjects are of a kind difficult to test. For instance, for the understanding of history and the appreciation of literature an interest in human affairs and an understanding of human nature are indispensable. In 1920, when the work was being planned, an attempt was made to find a test that should measure this. One was actually framed and used in a trial series and in 1921. In it the testees were given a number of passages taken from the conversation of three or four different characters. Each character was represented by three or more quotations. The testee was asked to group the quotations according to the characters they represented. The testee's criterion would be congruity of the behaviour described, or of the traits suggested. The characters were chosen from works of fiction, but the testees were not expected to recognize them. In selecting the quotations the experimenter tried to avoid introducing such marked peculiarities of style or diction as might afford a clue to the solution of the problem. The test was finally abandoned because the results correlated highly with the tests of general capacity and also because it was impossible to be sure that any system of marking was fair. For instance, if a testee arranges the quotations differently from their original connections, who is to say that the characters he thus implies are impossible, or even less probable than the originals?

Much that has been written in modern psychology suggests that there is a real distinction between individuals according to whether they are mainly interested in their fellows or turn away from them and interest themselves rather in the rest of nature (cf. Thorndike's social factor, and certain phases of the distinction between extrovert and introvert). If a real distinction can be drawn on this ground, or even if chance circumstances tend to marked specialization of interest along one line at the expense of the other, then one way of discovering the student likely to succeed in Arts rather than Science, might be to give a large number of topics or problems equally divided amongst the domains of human relations and the natural sciences, and ask him to attempt them in order of preference. Such a test would not be used to measure ability, but its results taken in relation to the student's performance on the tests of ability might be of considerable interest. We would surmise that a fundamental facility for language such as that measured by Test 2, together with a keen interest in human life and at least average general capacity in the sense of degree of confluence of experiences, are the main essentials for a successful Arts student. This opinion had been formed before *The Idea of Great Poetry*, by Lascelles Abercrombie, appeared. In it he claims as essentials for the poet just the factors that have been mentioned. The only difference being that in the case of language he speaks of incantation instead of mere facility. The incantation is essential for poetry in a way in which it is not for other Arts subjects, but even in the case of poetry it implies facility such as that measured by the test. His treatment of the other two factors may be illustrated from the following passage.

"What we recognize in great poetry is this unconfused complexity of rich experience, this confluence of all kinds of life into a single flame of consciousness, triumphantly asserting its luminous unity over all the manifold powers of its world. With Dante still in my mind, I take, to illustrate my theme further, and in objective substance, the first incident that occurs to me when I think of The Divine Comedy: an incident the more to my purpose for being so well known. The superb Farinata, as Dante approaches him, lifts himself erect out of his agony among the damned, 'as though he had hell in great scorn'; and abruptly and contemptuously greets the poet with the question, 'Who were thy ancestors?' At Dante's answer, he raises his eyebrows a little and says, 'They were my fierce adversaries, and I broke them twice.' And what a compound of the immortal grandeur and folly of human pride lives before us there! It is in this sort of life, in this concentrated wealth of simultaneous impression, with its allusion all round to all sorts of experience, that we move continually throughout The Divine Comedy."

Prof. Abercrombie argues that the confluence is present in all poetry, but to differing degrees, and that the degree of confluence is the measure of the greatness of the poetry. He shows, too, that it is in characterization and the understanding of human nature that the highest degree of confluence is essential. Upon this and the fact that the one test of characterization that was used correlated highly with general capacity, we may suggest the hypothesis that good general intelligence is more necessary for work in the Arts faculty than for work in the Science faculty. At the same time, the student with good general intelligence who lacks interest in human nature is not likely to succeed in Arts, because he does not gain familiarity with the essential material, the "humanities." For original work in science good general capacity is, of course, essential, but inasmuch as the material of the natural sciences is less complex than that of the humanities, it seems at least probable that a student who would have difficulty in Arts through comparatively low general capacity, might succeed in the sciences if he had developed the special abilities involved.

INDEX

Printed in Great Britain by
Butler & Tanner Ltd.,
Frome and London

For Product Safety Concerns and Information please contact our EU
representative GPSR@taylorandfrancis.com
Taylor & Francis Verlag GmbH, Kaufingerstraße 24, 80331 München, Germany

www.ingramcontent.com/pod-product-compliance
Ingram Content Group UK Ltd.
Pitfield, Milton Keynes, MK11 3LW, UK
UKHW022108190926
475702UK00013B/1328
* 9 7 8 1 8 4 8 7 2 2 5 1 4 *